Piano Chord Dictionary

All the essential chords in
an easy-to-follow format!

Alfred Music Co., Inc.
P.O. Box 10003
Van Nuys, CA 91410-0003
alfred.com

ISBN-10: 0-7390-9526-9
ISBN-13: 978-0-7390-9526-3

 Alfred Cares. Contents printed on environmentally responsible paper.

Contents

Introduction

Alfred's Mini Music Guide *Piano Chord Dictionary* provides the most essential chords and chordal information in a portable, handy size. Chords are listed alphabetically and chromatically for quick reference. On each page, the chord variations are arranged in a logical order with inversions and more complex extensions following simple triads. Within each key, the chords progress from the most basic major and minor chords all the way up to 7ths, 9ths, and even altered chords.

Each chord is shown in standard music notation and includes an illustrated keyboard diagram with fingerings and note names.

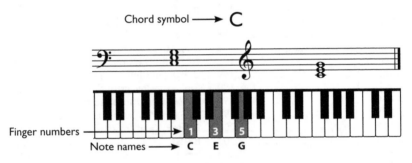

The fingers of both hands are numbered 1–5, starting with the thumb.

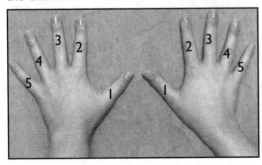

The first part of this book (pages 8–40) makes it easy to understand intervals and how chords are constructed. Theory on triads, seventh chords, extended chords, altered chords, and other chord types are covered.

The chords are only part of what you learn with this book. Once you are comfortable with the chords, you can refer to the Inversions and Advanced Voicing sections where you will learn about inversions, voicings, and voice leading to help you get the sound you want when playing chords. Once you understand voicings, you can take the chords in the book and use them to fit any performance situation. Try shell voicings, clusters, spread voicings, and even quartal voicings.

This book will provide the basis for an ever-growing chord vocabulary, an understanding of chord theory, and a fundamental knowledge of how chords are used in various musical styles.

Have fun!

Basic Intervals and Triads

Intervals

Chords are made up of three or more notes, and each note is a certain distance apart. We measure the distance between notes with *intervals* of a whole or half step.

A *half step* is the distance between any note and the closest black or white note on the keyboard either up or down. For example, the distance from C to C♯ is a half step. Similarly, the distance from E to F is a half step, and B to C is a half step.

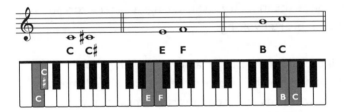

A *whole step* is the distance from any note to the closest note two half steps either up or down. For example, C to D is a whole step. Similarly, E to F♯ and B♭ to C are whole steps.

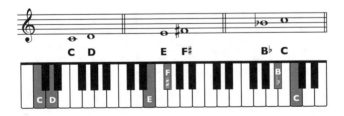

When you play a *scale*, you are playing intervals ordered in a specific way. A scale is simply an organization of whole steps and half steps. By understanding scales, you can easily create different chords. To create a major scale, we use the formula of whole, whole, half, whole, whole, whole, half. A C major scale is C, D, E, F, G, A, B, and C.

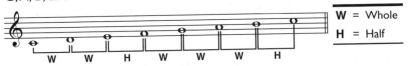

Each note of the scale represents a different scale degree. To determine the scale degree, number each note of the scale in order, with the first note being 1, and continue on with the numbers until you reach the last note, which is 8, or the *octave*.

The distance from C to D is a 2nd (C–D, 1–2), C to E is a 3rd (C–D–E, 1–2–3), C to F is a 4th (C–D–E–F, 1–2–3–4), and so on.

Intervals are not only labeled by the distance between scale degrees, but by the *quality* of the interval. An interval's quality is determined by counting the number of whole steps and half steps between the two notes of an interval. For example: C to E is a 3rd. C to E is also a major 3rd because there are 2 whole steps between C and E. Likewise, C to E♭ is also a 3rd, but C to E♭ is a minor 3rd because there are 1½ steps between C and E♭.

There are five qualities used to describe intervals: *major, minor, perfect, diminished*, and *augmented*. 5ths and octaves are called perfect intervals. When a minor 3rd or perfect 5th are lowered by a half step, they are called diminished. When a perfect interval is raised a half step, it is called augmented.

Following are abbreviations for the interval qualities.

M = Major

m = Minor

P = Perfect

o = Diminished (dim)

+ = Augmented (aug)

Triads

The most basic kind of chord is a *triad*, which is a chord made up of just three notes. There are four primary types of triads: major, minor, diminished, and augmented. Each triad is created from different combinations of intervals, and they all have a distinctly different sound. Triads are built by starting with the root and adding the note a 3rd above the root (the 3rd) and then another note a 3rd above the 3rd (the 5th).

The Major Triad
A *major triad* has a bright sound and is one of the most common chords in music. To create a major chord, use the formula of root (R), major 3rd (3), and 5th (5) of a major scale. The *root* is always the note of the chord for which the chord is named. For example, the root of a C major chord is the note C. You then add the 3rd, which is the interval of a 3rd above the root, and add another 3rd for the 5th of the chord. You can also think of a triad in half steps, where a major triad is made up of the root, the major 3rd, which is four half steps above the root, and the 5th, which is three half steps above the 3rd. Below is a C major triad:

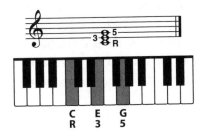

The Minor Triad

A *minor triad* has a dark sound and is a common chord in music. A minor triad is similar to the major triad, but the 3rd is one half step lower. To create a major chord, use the formula of root (R), minor 3rd (♭3), and 5th (5). When a 3rd is minor, that means it is lowered one half step. When you think of the minor chord in half steps, it includes a root, the minor 3rd, which is three half steps above the root, and the 5th, which is four half steps above the minor 3rd. Below is a C minor triad:

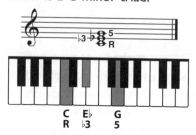

The Diminished Triad

A *diminished triad* has a very dark sound and is a not a very common chord, especially in popular music. A diminished triad is similar to the minor triad, but the 5th is one half step lower. To create a diminished chord, use the formula of root (R), minor 3rd (♭3), and diminished 5th (♭5). When a 5th is diminished, that means it is lowered one half step. When you think of the diminished chord in half steps, it includes a root, the minor 3rd, which is three half steps above the root, and the diminished 5th, which is three half steps above the minor 3rd. This symbol ° is often used to indicate a diminished interval or chord. Below is a C diminished triad:

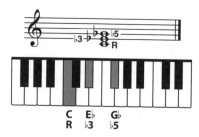

The Augmented Triad

An *augmented triad* has a very dissonant sound and is not a very common chord. An augmented triad is similar to the major triad, but the 5th is one half step higher. To create an augmented chord, use the formula of root (R), major 3rd (3), and augmented 5th (♯5). When a 5th is augmented, that means it is raised one half step. When you think of the augmented chord in half steps, it includes a root, the major 3rd, which is four half steps above the root, and the augmented 5th, which is four half steps above the minor 3rd. This symbol + is often used to indicate an augmented interval or chord. Below is a C augmented triad:

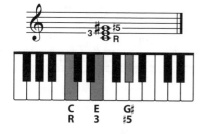

Table of Intervals

Below is a table of intervals starting on the note C. Notice that some intervals are labeled *enharmonic*, which means they are written differently but sound the same (for example, +2 and m3).

M = Major
m = Minor
+ = Augmented
o = Diminished

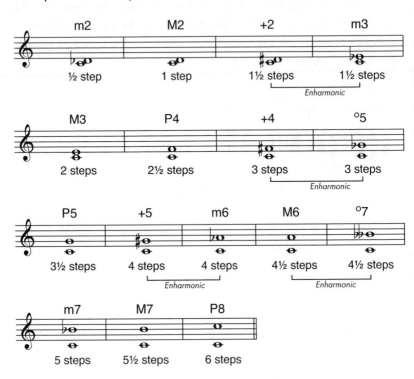

Seventh Chords

By stacking a 3rd on top of a triad, you create a *seventh chord*. There are five common seventh chords: *dominant seventh*, *minor seventh*, *major seventh*, *diminished seventh*, and the *minor seventh flat five*. All seventh chords consist of a triad with the addition of the 7th.

Dominant Seventh (7)

To create a dominant seventh chord, add a minor 3rd above the 5th of a major triad (C–E–G–B♭). The 7th of this chord is three half steps above the 5th. Here is a C dominant seventh chord:

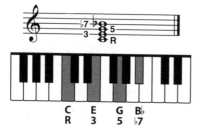

Minor Seventh (m7)

To create a minor seventh chord, add a minor 3rd above the 5th of a minor triad (C–E♭–G–B♭). The 7th of this chord is three half steps above the 5th. Here is a C minor seventh chord:

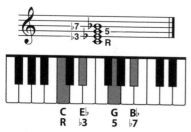

Major Seventh (maj7)

To create a major seventh chord, add a major 3rd above the 5th of a major triad (C–E–G–B). The 7th of this chord is 4 half steps above the 5th. Here is a C major seventh chord:

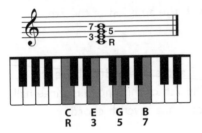

Diminished Seventh (°7)

To create a diminished seventh chord, add a minor 3rd above the 5th of a diminished triad (C–E♭–G♭–B♭♭). The B♭♭ is the enharmonic equivalent of A natural. The 7th of this chord is 3 half steps above the 5th. Here is a C diminished seventh chord:

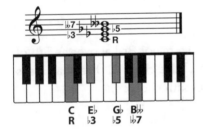

Minor Seventh Flat Five (m7♭5)

The minor seventh flat five chord is sometimes called a half-diminished seventh chord. To create a minor seventh flat five chord, add a major 3rd above the 5th of a diminished triad (C–E♭–G♭–B♭). You can also think of it as a dominant seventh chord with the 5th and 3rd lowered a half step (diminished). The 7th of this chord is 4 half steps above the 5th. Here is a C minor seventh flat five chord:

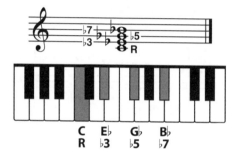

Extended Chords

As you have learned, basic triads are built by stacking 3rds.
You've also learned that adding an additional 3rd will create a
7th chord. When we continue to add 3rds beyond the 7th, we
create *extended* chords.

The most common extensions beyond the 7th are the 9th, 11th,
and 13th. We can find these notes easily by building a two-octave
major scale. Giving each note in the scale a number, it easy to find
the extensions: 9, 11, and 13.

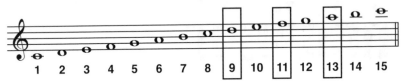

Notice also that these extensions are simply versions of the 2nd,
4th, and 6th—only one octave higher.

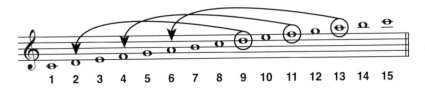

So, it's also easy to make new chords by adding the extensions on top of a 7th chord. Here are some common extended chords:

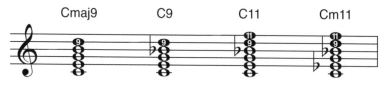

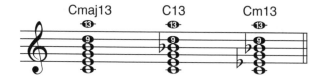

The tones 9, 11, and 13 are never referred to as 2, 4, or 6 when the chord also contains the 3rd and the 7th. This is not difficult to remember…just keep in mind that if the 7th is present and there are notes other than the root, 3rd, 5th, or 7th, then it is an extended harmony and the additional notes will be numbered higher than 7.

The most common extended chords are:

Major 9	=	maj9
Minor 9	=	m9
Dominant 9	=	9
Minor 11	=	m11

Dominant 11	=	11
Major 13	=	maj13
Minor 13	=	m13
Dominant 13	=	13

Here are a couple of important things to remember: Major 11 chords are rarely used because the 11th (4th) clashes with the major 3rd; 11ths are usually omitted from 13th chords for the same reason. Often, the 11th is sharped (♯11, same as a ♭5, see Altered Chords, page 22) to avoid this clash.

Other Chord Types
Sus Chords

The common triads can be changed to create tension or color in music. One of the most common ways to add interest to a chord is to replace the 3rd with either a 2nd or 4th. These are called *sus chords*.

For example, if we replace the 3rd of a major triad with a 2nd, we create a *sus2 chord*. If we replace the 3rd with a 4th, we create a *sus4 chord*.

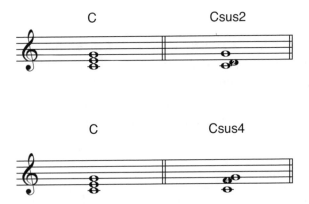

Remember, the point is to replace the 3rd...if the 3rd were also present, then we would be creating something else.

Add Chords

If the 3rd is present and a 2nd is added, we think of it as a 9th, and the resulting chord is an *add9* chord. If the 3rd is present and we add a 4th, we think of it as an 11th, and the chord is an *add11* chord. As in the extended chords, a major add11 is rarely used because of the clash between the 11th (4th) and the 3rd.

5 Chords (Power Chords)

Eliminating the 3rd altogether and retaining just the root and the 5th creates a *5 chord*, sometimes called a *power chord*. Since there is no 3rd, a 5 chord is neither major or minor. Classical musicians think of this as being an "open" sound, and rock musicians use them for pretty much the same reason; powerful, yet undefined, a 5 chord can be combined with many different kinds of sounds. The root is often doubled in a 5 chord.

6th Chords

6th chords are similar to 7th chords in that they are four-note chords. The 6th is added to the triad. A 6th is a great color to add to both major and minor triads.

Altered Chords

Raising or lowering a note in a chord by using an *accidental* (sharp, flat, or natural) is called making an *alteration*. We don't use this term for changing one basic triad into another type (e.g., lowering the 3rd of a major chord to create a minor chord). Rather, an altered chord is an extended chord where the 5th or 9th is raised or lowered with an accidental. Doing this adds a *non-diatonic* note (a note not belonging to the key) to the chord and thus creates a lot of tension, which is the whole point. Major, minor, and dominant chords may be altered, but it is most common to alter dominant chords.

Only 5ths or 9ths can be altered. Altering any other note can be interpreted as an altered 5th or 9th. The following chart shows how any chord alteration can be interpreted as altering the 5th or 9th. Enharmonic relationships are important to these interpretations.

Altered Scale Tone		Alteration
Raising the root	=	♭9
Lowering the 2nd or 9th	=	♭9
Raising the 2nd or 9th	=	♯9
Lowering the 3rd	=	♯9
Raising the 3rd	=	4th or 11th, not an alteration
Lowering the 4th or 11th	=	3rd, not an alteration
Raising the 4th or 11th	=	♭5
Lowering the 5th	=	♭5
Raising the 5th	=	♯5
Lowering the 6th or 13th	=	♯5
Raising the 6th or 13th	=	♭7, essential dominant chord tone, not an alteration
Lowering the 7th	=	♭7, essential dominant chord tone, not an alteration
Raising the 7th	=	root

Altered Dominant Chords

Here are the four basic altered dominant chords, and four ways to alter both the 5th and 9th in a dominant chord:

Inversions

Inverted Triads

When a chord is played with the root as the lowest note, it is called a *root position chord*. When a note other than the root is the lowest note, the chord is an *inversion*. The position of notes in the chord is called the *voicing*.

Sometimes, you will use an inversion to have a note other than the root in the bass. Other times, you may use an inversion to have a particular note at the top of the chord. Depending on the inversion, you will have the option of choosing which note is on the top or bottom of that chord. The chord is still the same, but it will sound different in different inversions.

Root Position

There are three positions possible for a triad: root position, first inversion, and second inversion. When the lowest note is the root, the chord is in root position.

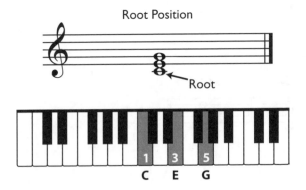

24

First Inversion

When the lowest note is the 3rd of the chord, the chord is in first inversion.

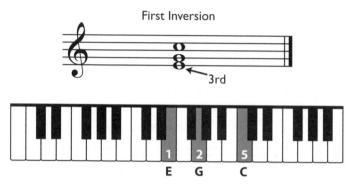

First Inversion

Second Inversion

When the lowest note is the 5th of the chord, the chord is in second inversion.

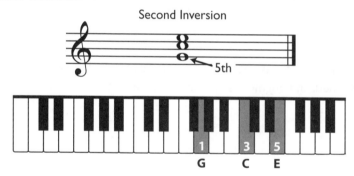

Second Inversion

The method for inverting triads is the same for major, minor, diminished, and augmented triads. Root position always has the root in the bass, first inversion has the 3rd in the bass, and second inversion has the 5th in the bass.

Inverted Seventh Chords

Root position, first inversion, and second inversion voicings of
seventh chords have the same notes as the lowest notes—root, 3rd
and 5th.

Third Inversion
When inverting seventh chords, there is a fourth note in the chord,
so there is another inversion possible. When the 7th is the lowest
note, it is called the third inversion.

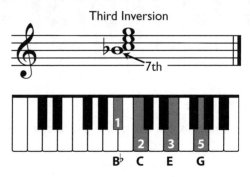

Inverting sevenths is the same for dominant, minor, major,
diminished, and augmented seventh chords.

Two-Hand Voicings

Some chords have more notes than you can comfortably play with one hand. In that case, you will voice the notes using two hands. To comfortably play the C7♭9 chord, the lower three notes are played with the left hand and the upper two notes are played with the right hand. Two-hand voicings will be needed for many of the extended chords.

The photo below shows the two-handed voicing of C7♭9. Notice in the keyboard diagram underneath the photo that the left and right hands are indicated with this mark ⌐ or this mark ⌐ underneath the finger numbers.

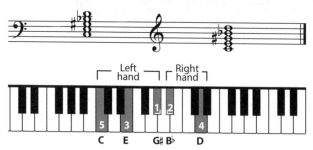

Because there are so many inversions possible with extended chords, only root position chords are shown in this book, but you may experiment with different voicings to get different sounds.

Voice Leading

The voicing possibilities are seemingly endless, especially for chords
with more than four notes. When voicing chords, it is important
that the chord sounds good and fits with the melody you are
playing. You also need to consider that when moving from chord to
chord, there are voicing options that are smoother than others. For
example, when playing a C7 chord to an F chord, you could play
both chords in root position like this:

But a smooth way to voice those two chords is to play the C7
in root position and the F chord in second inversion. This sounds
better and reduces the motion of your hand.

Voicing for the Melody

Using the correct inversion will allow you to keep the melody of a song on the top of the harmony. By changing the inversion of the chords appropriately, the melody can always remain the highest-sounding note. Below is an example of "Jingle Bells" where the melody is on top. Notice that four different inversions are used.

Jingle Bells

Second inversion .... Root First Third Second

Advanced Voicings

Shell Voicings

A *shell* is sort of a "bare bones" approach to playing a chord and is a type of *rootless voicing*. Shell voicings are played with just the 3rd and the 7th (leaving out the root), as these are the two tones that define the essential chord type. For example, for Cmaj7, play just E (3) and B (7). For Cm7, play just E♭ (♭3)and B♭ (♭7). Play the note C to get the root "in your ear," then play the two shells. You'll see that the shell is enough to convey the idea of the chord.

Clusters

A *cluster* is a group of two or more notes played very close together, usually just a whole or half step apart. Because the notes are so close together, there is always some clashing, or *dissonance*.

To create a cluster, find two notes in a chord from among the fundamental chord tones (root, 3rd, 5th, 6th, or 7th), the extensions (9th, 11th, 13th), and altered tones, that can be played a whole step apart.

Clusters in Whole Steps

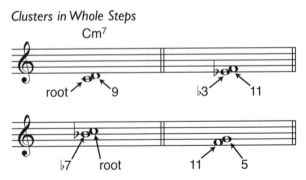

You can also create clusters using half steps.

Clusters in Half Steps

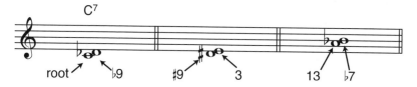

Obviously, since you're only playing two notes, you're only hinting at the chord, not actually playing it. Another option is to begin with the shell voicing for the chord and then squeeze additional extensions and alterations between and around the two notes.

Spread Voicings

A *spread voicing* is one where the notes of the chord have been spread out, played further apart, than usual. Look at the three voicings below.

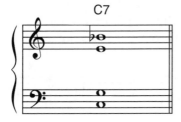

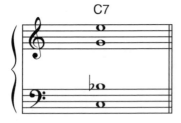

The first voicing on the previous page is a basic root–3–5–♭7 voicing. In the second voicing, 3 and ♭7 are moved up an octave. In the third, 5 is moved up an octave and 3 is moved up two octaves. All three are C7, yet they have very different sounds. A spread voicing is a good way to make a chord sound more full and rich. It is also a good way to emphasize a particular note in the chord, such as the way the third voicing emphasizes the 3rd by putting it on top.

Be careful with the use of spread voicings. It is possible to spread a voicing so wide that the notes no longer sound like a unified chord. For example, play this one:

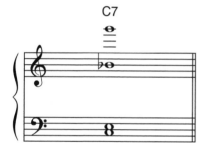

Remember that it is generally a good idea to use the fundamental chord tones—the 3rd and 7th—in the lower part of a spread voicing. It will help establish the chord's identity for the listener.

Quartal (4th) Voicings

A *quartal,* or *4th, voicing,* is one based on perfect 4ths. We ordinarily think in terms of 3rds: we stack 3rds to make triads and 7th chords, adding additional 3rds to find the extensions. With quartal voicings, we're not going to dispose of our *tertian* (based on 3rds) harmonic system; we're just going to use perfect 4ths to create some interesting sounds. For example, the following Cm11 and Cmaj13 chords:

Cm11

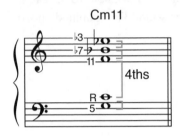

Cmaj13

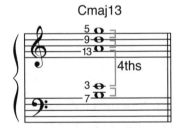

It is not always possible to use perfect 4ths exclusively and still play normal chord types. A chord with mostly perfect 4ths is still considered quartal, as in the examples below.

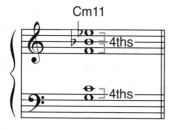

Chord Symbol Variations

Chord symbols are a form of musical shorthand that give musicians as much information about a chord as quickly as possible. Since chord symbols are not universally standardized, they are often written in many different ways—some are understandable, others are confusing. To illustrate this point, below is a listing of some of the ways copyists, composers, and arrangers have created variations on the more common chord symbols. The left column (Symbol) shows the chord symbols used in this book, the middle column (Type) gives the quality of the chord, and the right column (Alternate Symbols) shows some variations. Note that this chart is only offered as a representative list, but it should help you interpret any chord symbol you come across.

Symbol	Type	Alternate Symbols
C	Major	CM, Cmaj, C△, C Major
Cm	Minor	C-, Cmin, Cmi.
C°	Diminished	Cdim, Cm(♭5), Cmin(♭5), C-(♭5)
C+	Augmented	Caug, C(♯5)
Csus4	Suspended	Csus, C(addF), C4
Csus2	Suspended	sus2, C(addD), C2
C(♭5)	Altered Major	C(-5)

Symbol	Type	Alternate Symbols
C5	Open	C(no3), C(omit3)
C6	Major	Cmaj6, C(addA), C(A)
C7	Dominant	C(addB♭), C7̸, C(-7), C(+7)
C°7	Diminished	Cdim7, C7dim
Cmaj7	Major	CM7, C△7
Cm6	Minor	C-6, Cm(addA), Cm(+6)
Cm7	Minor	Cmi7, Cmin7, C-7, C7mi
Cm11	Minor	C-11, Cm(♭11), Cmi7$^{11}_{9}$, C-7($^{9}_{11}$)
Cm7(♭5)	Half-Diminished	Cmin7♭5, Cmi7-5, C-7(5-), Cø7, C½dim
Cmaj7(♭5)	Altered Major	Cmaj7(-5), C7(-5), C△7(♭5)
Cm(maj7)	Harmonic Minor	C-maj7, C-7̸, Cmi7̸
C7(♭5)	Altered Dominant	C7-5, C7(5-), C7(♯4)

Symbol	Type	Alternate Symbols
C7(♯5)	Altered Dominant	C7+, C7+5, C7(5+), C7aug, C7aug5
C7(♭9)	Altered Dominant	C7(-9), C9♭, C9-
C7(♯9)	Altered Dominant	C7(+9), C9♯ , C9♯
C7(♭5♭9)	Altered Dominant	C7♭5♭9, C$_{-5}^{♭9}$
C7(♯5♭9)	Altered Dominant	C7+(♭9), Caug7-9, C+7(♭9), C+9♭, C+9♭
C7(♯5♯9)	Altered Dominant	C9+, C9(+5), Caug9, C(♯9♯5), C+9
C7sus4	Dominant	C7sus, Csus7, C7(+4)
C9	Dominant	C⁹, C7add9, C7(addD), C7(+9)
C9(♭5)	Altered Dominant	C9(-5), C7$_{-5}^{9}$, C9(5♭)
C9(♯11)	Altered Dominant	C9(+11), C(♯11), C11+, C11♯
C11	Dominant	C9(11), C9addF, C9+11, C7$_{11}^{9}$

Symbol	Type	Alternate Symbols
C(add9)	Suspended	C(9), C(add2), C(+9), C(+D)
C13	Dominant	C9addA, C9(6), C7addA, C7+A
C13(♭9)	Altered Dominant	C13(-9), C$^{13}_{♭9}$, C(♭9)addA
Cmaj9	Major	C♯7(9), C♯7(+9), C9(maj7), C/9
C6/9	Major	C6(add9), C6(addD), C9(no7), C9/6
Cm6/9	Minor	C-6/9, Cm6(+9), Cm6(add9), Cm6(+D)
Cm9	Minor	Cm7(9), Cm7(+9), C-9, Cmi7(9+)
C13(♭5♭9)	Altered Dominant	C13($^{♭9}_{♭5}$), C13(-9-5), C(♭9♭5)addA
Cm9(maj7)	Harmonic Minor	C-9(♯7), C(-9)♯7, Cmi9(♯7)

Circle of 5ths

The circle of 5ths will help to clarify which chords are enharmonic equivalents (notice that chords can be written enharmonically as well as notes). The circle of 5ths also serves as a quick reference guide to the relationship of the keys and how key signatures can be figured out. Clockwise movement (up a P5) provides all of the sharp keys by adding one sharp to the key signature. Counterclockwise (down a P5) provides the flat keys by adding one flat.

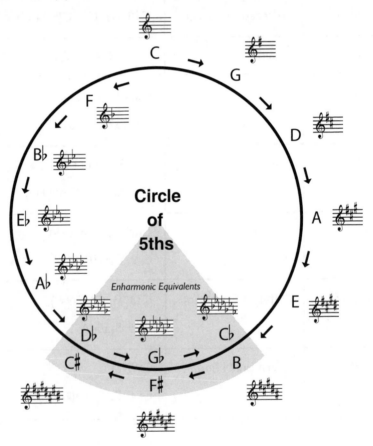

Chords in All 12 Keys

C

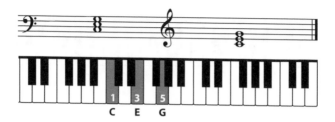

C (1ST INVERSION)

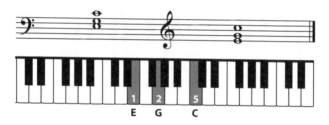

C (2ND INVERSION)

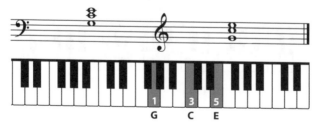

Cm

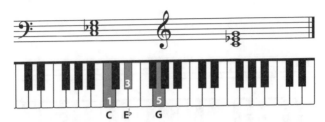

Cm (1ST INVERSION)

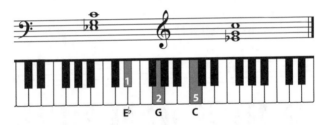

Cm (2ND INVERSION)

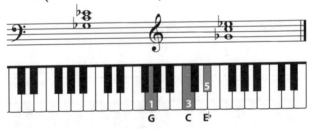

C°

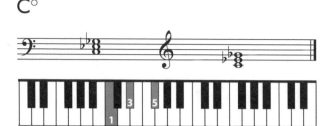

C° (1st inversion)

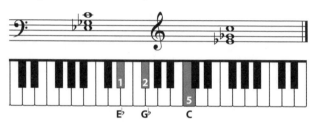

C° (2nd inversion)

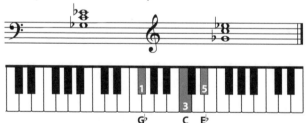

C+

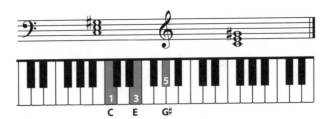

C+ (1ST INVERSION)

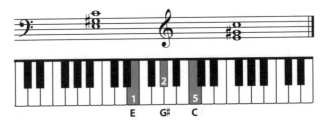

C+ (2ND INVERSION)

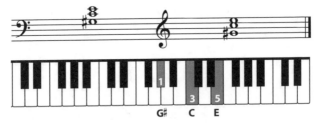

Csus2

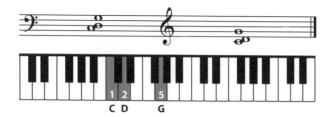

Csus4

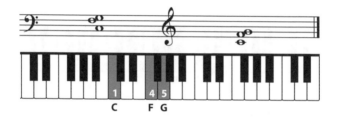

C5 (POWER CHORD)

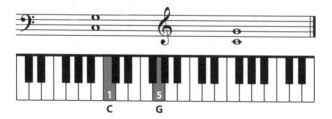

C6

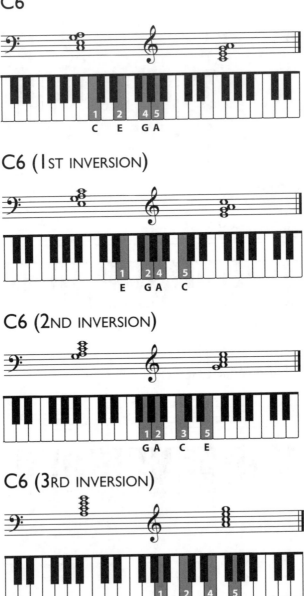

C6 (1ST INVERSION)

C6 (2ND INVERSION)

C6 (3RD INVERSION)

Cm6

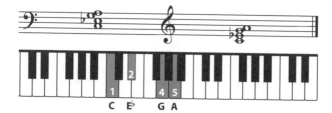

C E♭ G A

Cm6 (1ST INVERSION)

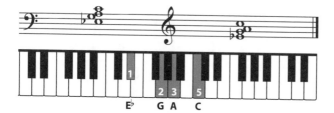

E♭ G A C

Cm6 (2ND INVERSION)

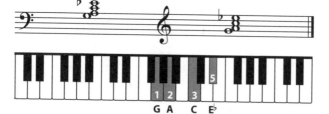

G A C E♭

Cm6 (3RD INVERSION)

A C E♭ G

C7

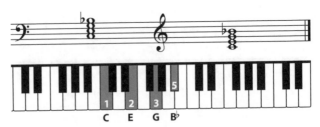

C E G B♭

C7 (1ST INVERSION)

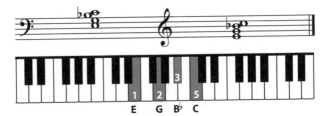

E G B♭ C

C7 (2ND INVERSION)

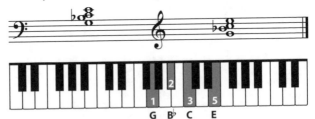

G B♭ C E

C7 (3RD INVERSION)

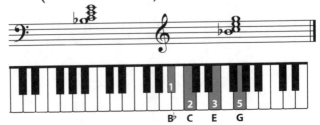

B♭ C E G

Cmaj7

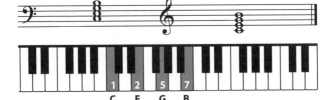

C E G B

Cmaj7 (1ST INVERSION)

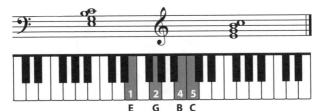

E G B C

Cmaj7 (2ND INVERSION)

G B C E

Cmaj7 (3RD INVERSION)

B C E G

C

C

Cm7

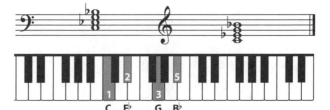

Cm7 (1ST INVERSION)

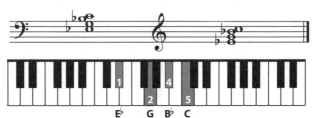

Cm7 (2ND INVERSION)

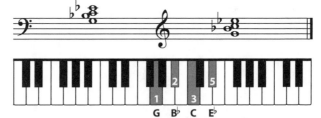

Cm7 (3RD INVERSION)

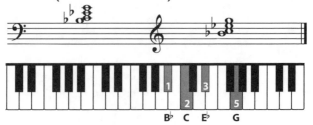

Cm7(♭5)

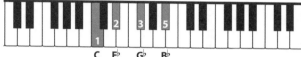

C E♭ G♭ B♭

Cm7(♭5) (1ST INVERSION)

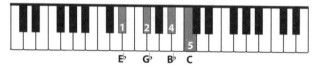

E♭ G♭ B♭ C

Cm7(♭5) (2ND INVERSION)

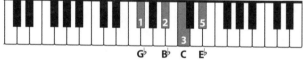

G♭ B♭ C E♭

Cm7(♭5) (3RD INVERSION)

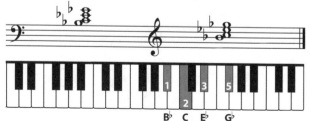

B♭ C E♭ G♭

C°7

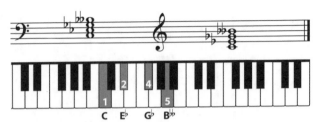

C E♭ G♭ B♭♭

C°7 (1ST INVERSION)

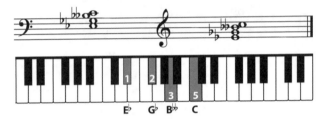

E♭ G♭ B♭♭ C

C°7 (2ND INVERSION)

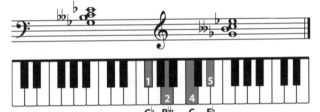

G♭ B♭♭ C E♭

C°7 (3RD INVERSION)

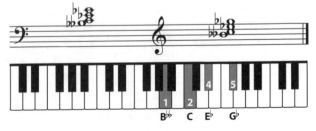

B♭♭ C E♭ G♭

C(add9)*

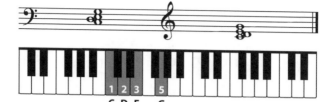

1 2 3 5
C D E G

C(add9)* (1ST INVERSION)

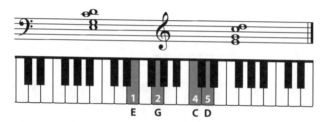

1 2 4 5
E G C D

C(add9)* (2ND INVERSION)

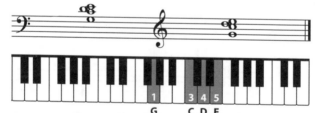

1 3 4 5
G C D E

C(add9)* (3RD INVERSION)

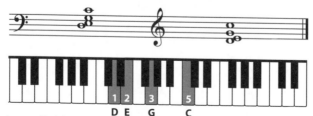

1 2 3 5
D E G C

* Sometimes called (add2)

C

C9

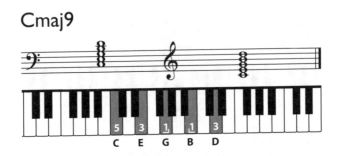

C E G B♭ D

Cmaj9

C E G B D

Cm9

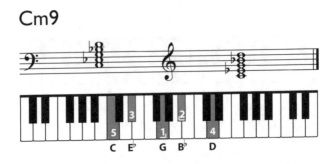

C E♭ G B♭ D

Cmaj7(♭5)

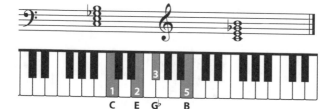

C E G♭ B

Cmaj7(♯5)

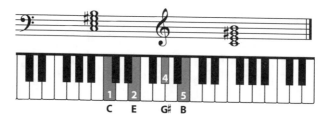

C E G♯ B

C7(♭5)

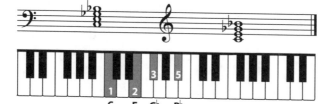

C E G♭ B♭

C7(♯5)

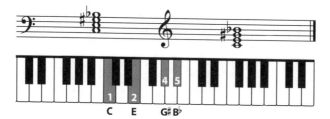

C E G♯ B♭

C7(♭9)

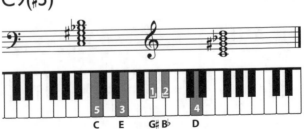

C E G B♭ D♭

C7(♯9)

C E G B♭ D♯

C9(♭5)

C E G♭ B♭ D

C9(♯5)

C E G♯ B♭ D

C#

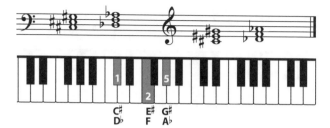

C# (1st INVERSION)

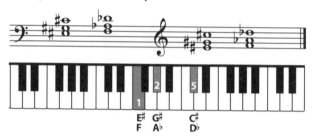

C# (2nd INVERSION)

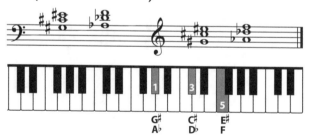

C#m

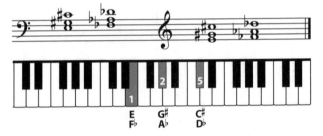

C# E   G#
D♭ F♭ A♭

C#m (1st inversion)

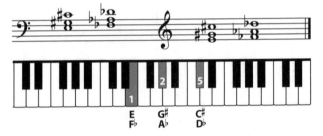

E   G# C#
F♭ A♭ D♭

C#m (2nd inversion)

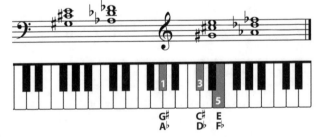

G# C# E
A♭ D♭ F♭

C#°

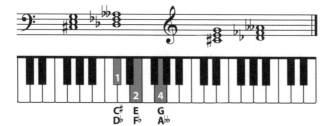

C#
D♭   E   G
     F♭ A♭♭

C#° (1ST INVERSION)

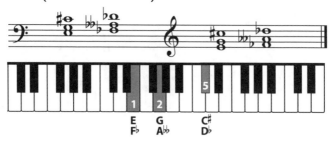

E   G   C#
F♭ A♭♭   D♭

C#° (2ND INVERSION)

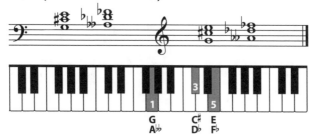

G   C# E
A♭♭   D♭ F♭

59

C#+

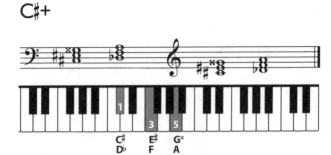

C#
D♭

C#+ (1st inversion)

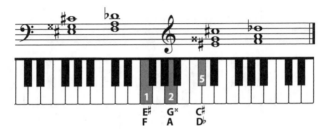

C#+ (2nd inversion)

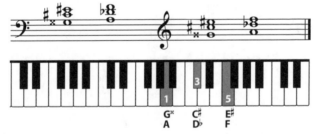

C#sus2

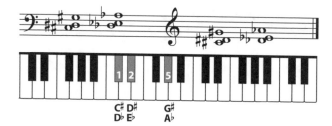

C# D#
Db Eb

G#
Ab

C#sus4

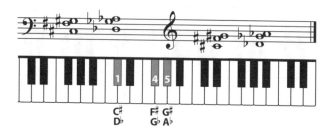

C#
Db

F# G#
Gb Ab

C#5 (POWER CHORD)

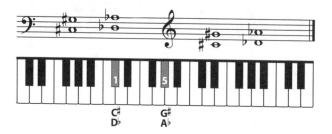

C#
Db

G#
Ab

C#6

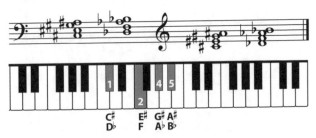

C#6 (1ST INVERSION)

C#6 (2ND INVERSION)

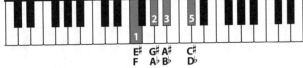

C#6 (3RD INVERSION)

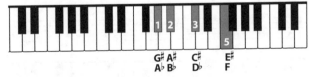
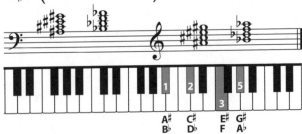

C#m6

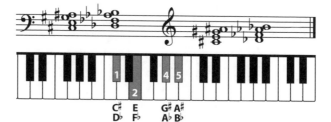

C# E   G# A#
Db Fb Ab Bb

C#m6 (1ST INVERSION)

E   G# A# C#
Fb Ab Bb Db

C#m6 (2ND INVERSION)

G# A# C# E
Ab Bb Db Fb

C#m6 (3RD INVERSION)

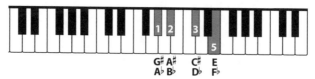

A# C# E   G#
Bb Db Fb Ab

C#7

C#7 (1ST INVERSION)

C#7 (2ND INVERSION)

C#7 (3RD INVERSION)

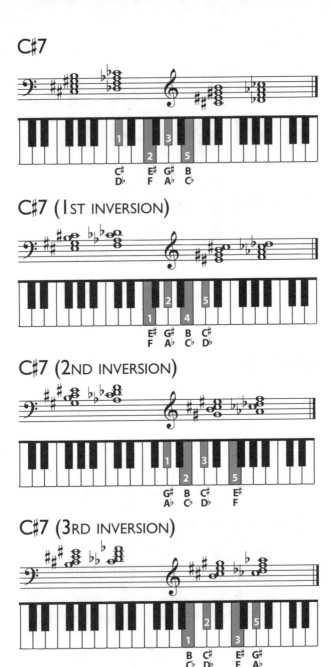

C#maj7

C#
D♭

C#maj7 (1ST INVERSION)

C#maj7 (2ND INVERSION)

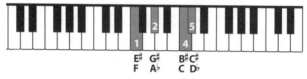

C#maj7 (3RD INVERSION)

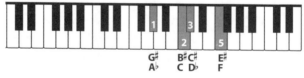

C#m7

C# E   G# B
Db Fb Ab Cb

C#m7 (1ST INVERSION)

E   G# B   C#
Fb Ab Cb Db

C#m7 (2ND INVERSION)

G# B   C# E
Ab Cb Db Fb

C#m7 (3RD INVERSION)

B   C# E   G#
Cb Db Fb Ab

C#m7(♭5)

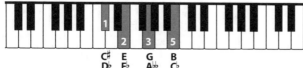

C# E   G   B
D♭ F♭ A♭♭ C♭

C#m7(♭5) (1ST INVERSION)

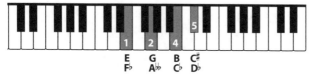

E   G   B   C#
F♭ A♭♭ C♭ D♭

C#m7(♭5) (2ND INVERSION)

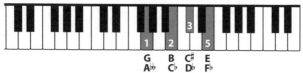

G   B   C# E
A♭♭ C♭ D♭ F♭

C#m7(♭5) (3RD INVERSION)

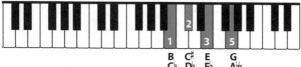

B   C# E   G
C♭ D♭ F♭ A♭♭

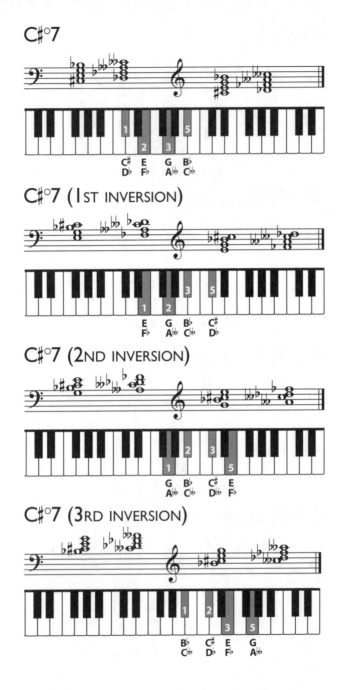

C#(add9)*

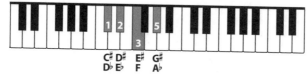

C# D# E# G#
Db Eb F Ab

C#(add9)* (1ST INVERSION)

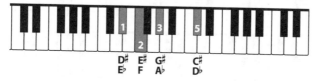

D# E# G# C#
Eb F Ab Db

C#(add9)* (2ND INVERSION)

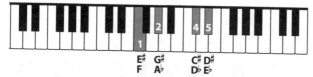

E# G# C# D#
F Ab Db Eb

C#(add9)* (3RD INVERSION)

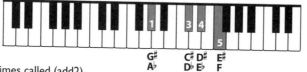

G# C# D# E#
Ab Db Eb F

* Sometimes called (add2)

C#
Db

C#9

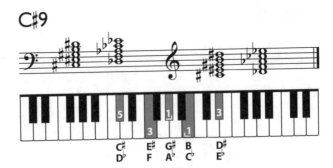

C#maj9

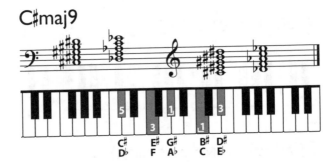

C#m9

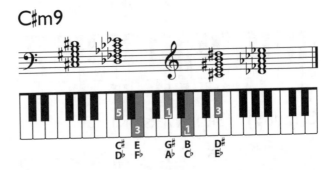

C#maj7(b5)

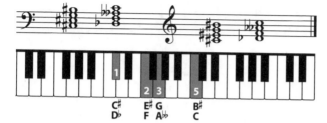

C#/Db

C#maj7(#5)

C#7(b5)

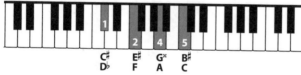

C#7(#5)

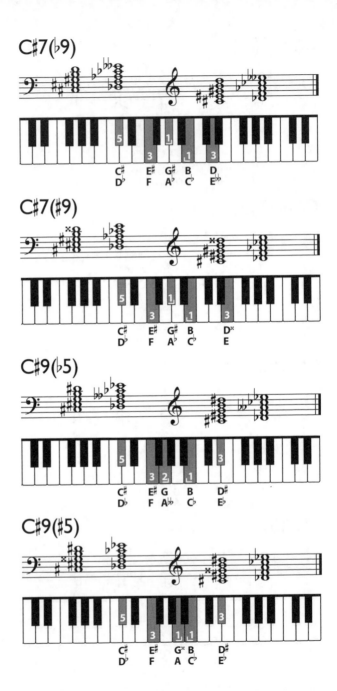

D

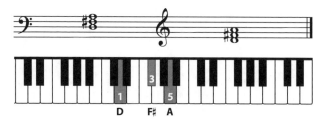

D   F♯   A

D (1ST INVERSION)

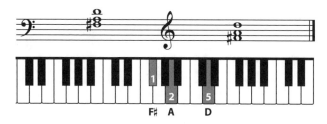

F♯   A   D

D (2ND INVERSION)

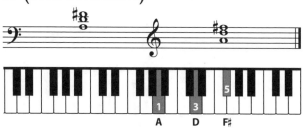

A   D   F♯

Dm

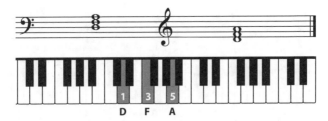

D F A

Dm (1ST INVERSION)

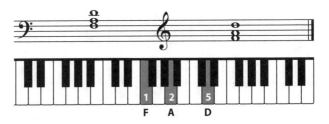

F A D

Dm (2ND INVERSION)

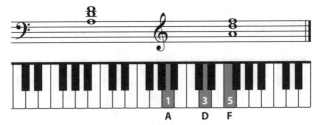

A D F

D

D°

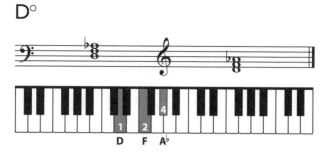

D° (1ST INVERSION)

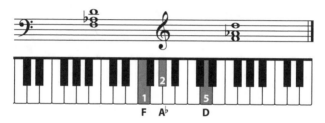

D° (2ND INVERSION)

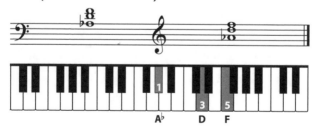

D

D+

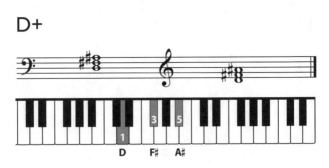

D+ (1ST INVERSION)

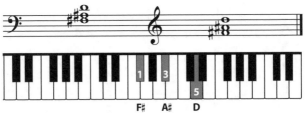

D+ (2ND INVERSION)

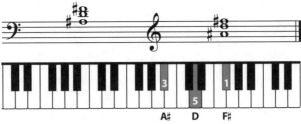

Dsus2

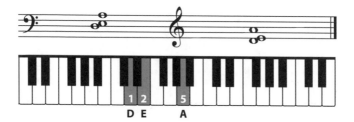

D E   A

Dsus4

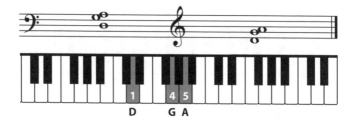

D   G A

D5 (POWER CHORD)

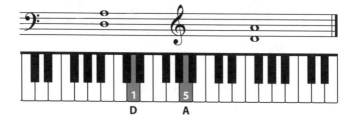

D   A

D6

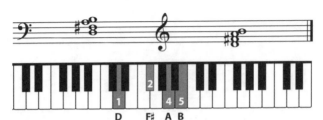

D   F# A B

D6 (1ST INVERSION)

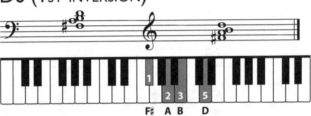

F# A B D

D6 (2ND INVERSION)

A B D F#

D6 (3RD INVERSION)

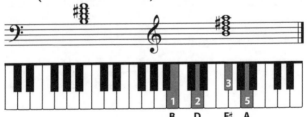

B D F# A

D

Dm6

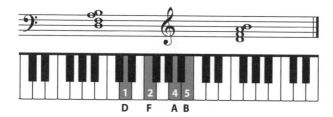

D F A B

Dm6 (1ST INVERSION)

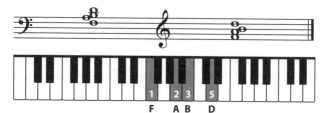

F A B D

Dm6 (2ND INVERSION)

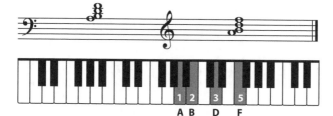

A B D F

Dm6 (3RD INVERSION)

B D F A

D7

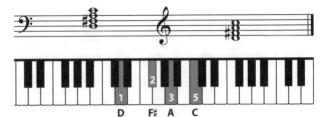

D   F# A   C

D7 (1ST INVERSION)

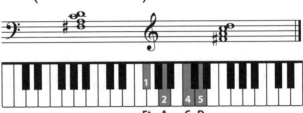

F# A   C D

D7 (2ND INVERSION)

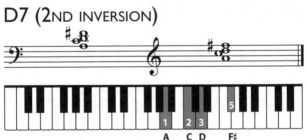

A   C D   F#

D7 (3RD INVERSION)

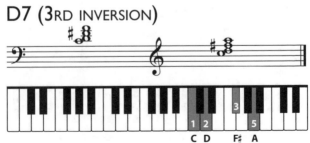

C D   F# A

Dmaj7

Dmaj7 (1ST INVERSION)

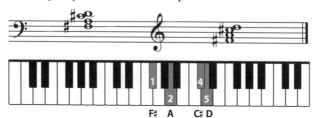

Dmaj7 (2ND INVERSION)

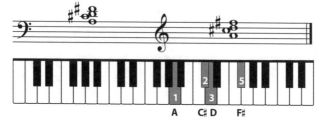

Dmaj7 (3RD INVERSION)

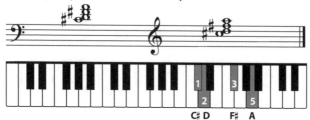

D

Dm7

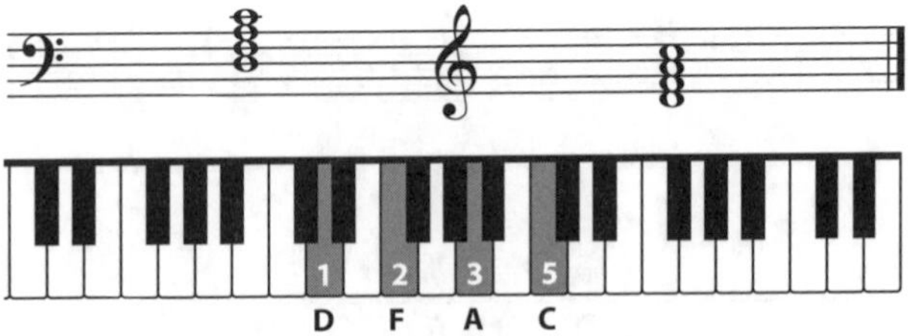

D F A C

Dm7 (1st inversion)

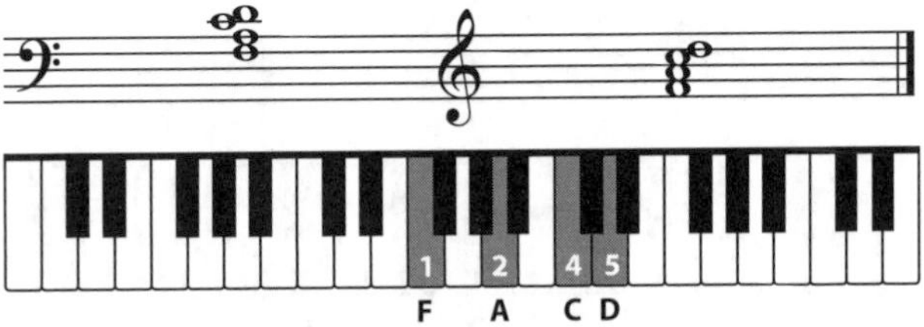

F A C D

Dm7 (2nd inversion)

A C D F

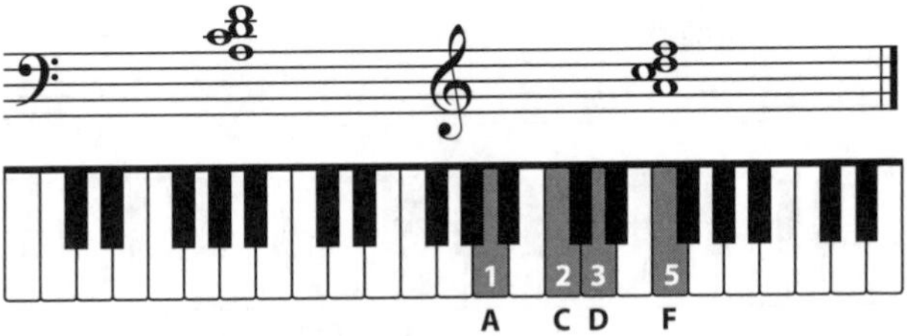

Dm7 (3rd inversion)

C D F A

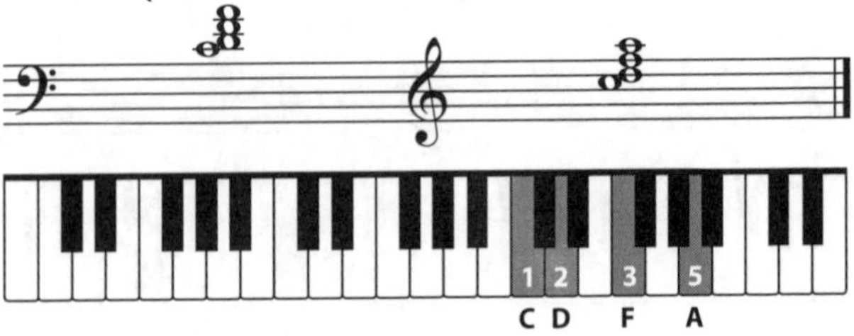

Dm7(♭5)

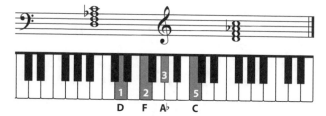

D F A♭ C

Dm7(♭5) (1ST INVERSION)

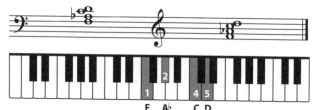

F A♭ C D

Dm7(♭5) (2ND INVERSION)

A♭ C D F

Dm7(♭5) (3RD INVERSION)

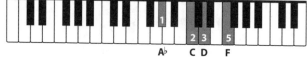

C D F A♭

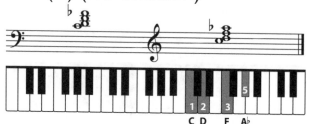

D°7

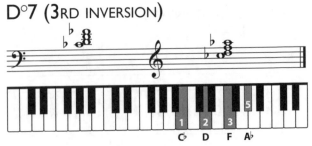

D°7 (1ST INVERSION)

D°7 (2ND INVERSION)

D°7 (3RD INVERSION)

D(add9)*

D E F# A

D(add9)* (1ST INVERSION)

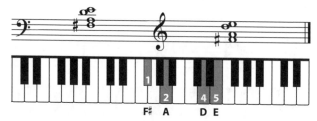

F# A   D E

D(add9)* (2ND INVERSION)

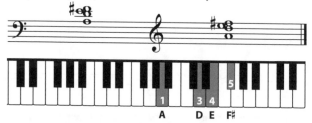

A   D E F#

D(add9)* (3RD INVERSION)

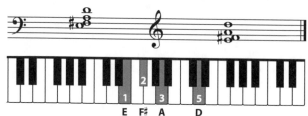

E F# A   D

* Sometimes called (add2)

D

D9

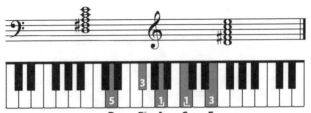

D F# A C E

Dmaj9

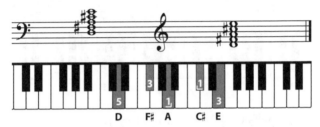

D F# A C# E

Dm9

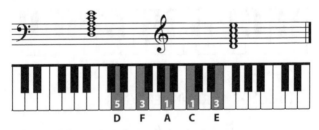

D F A C E

Dmaj7(♭5)

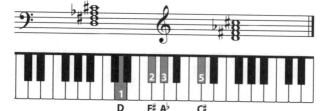

Dmaj7(♯5)

D7(♭5)

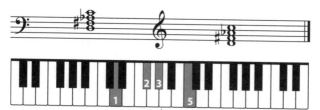

D7(♯5)

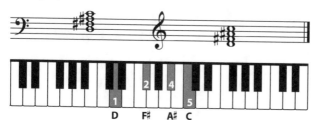

D

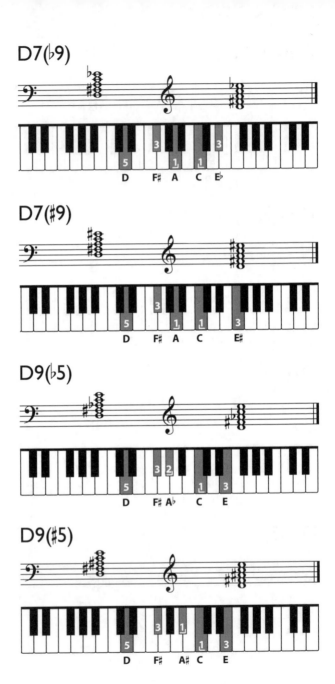

E♭

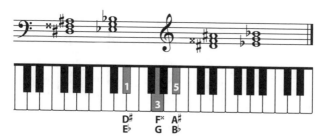

D♯   F×   A♯
E♭   G   B♭

E♭ (1ST INVERSION)

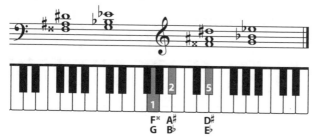

F×   A♯   D♯
G   B♭   E♭

E♭ (2ND INVERSION)

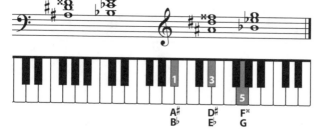

A♯   D♯   F×
B♭   E♭   G

E♭m

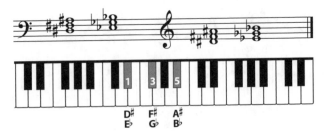

E♭m (1ST INVERSION)

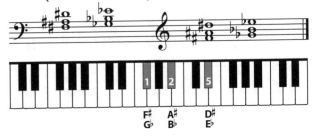

E♭m (2ND INVERSION)

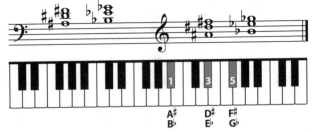

E♭°

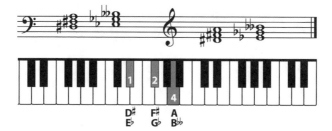

D#
Eb

E♭° (1ST INVERSION)

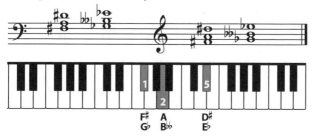

E♭° (2ND INVERSION)

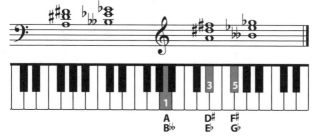

E♭+

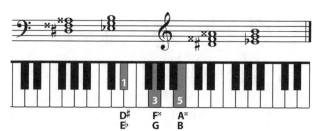

D♯ / E♭

E♭+ (1ST INVERSION)

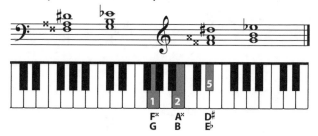

E♭+ (2ND INVERSION)

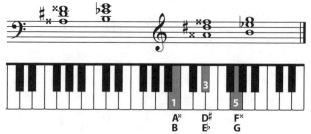

E♭sus2

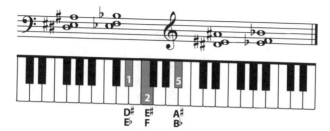

E♭sus4

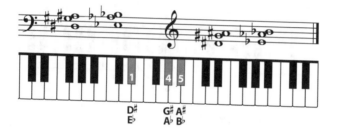

E♭5 (POWER CHORD)

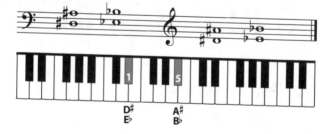

E♭6

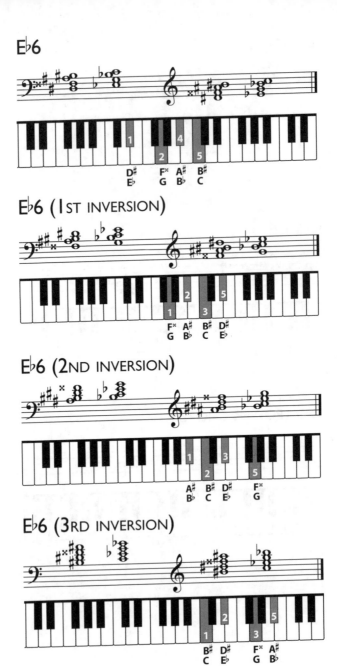

E♭6 (1ST INVERSION)

E♭6 (2ND INVERSION)

E♭6 (3RD INVERSION)

D#
E♭

E♭m6

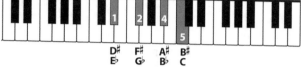

D♯	F♯	A♯	B♯
E♭	G♭	B♭	C

E♭m6 (1ST INVERSION)

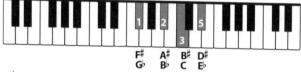

F♯	A♯	B♯	D♯
G♭	B♭	C	E♭

E♭m6 (2ND INVERSION)

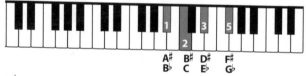

A♯	B♯	D♯	F♯
B♭	C	E♭	G♭

E♭m6 (3RD INVERSION)

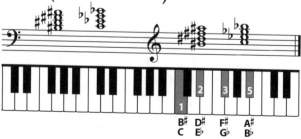

B♯	D♯	F♯	A♯
C	E♭	G♭	B♭

E♭7

D♯   F×   A♯   C♯
E♭   G   B♭   D♭

E♭7 (1ST INVERSION)

F×   A♯   C♯   D♯
G   B♭   D♭   E♭

E♭7 (2ND INVERSION)

A♯   C♯   D♯   F×
B♭   D♭   E♭   G

E♭7 (3RD INVERSION)

C♯   D♯   F×   A♯
D♭   E♭   G   B♭

E♭maj7

E♭maj7 (1ST INVERSION)

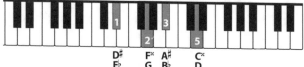

E♭maj7 (2ND INVERSION)

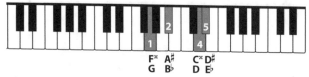

E♭maj7 (3RD INVERSION)

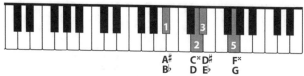

E♭m7

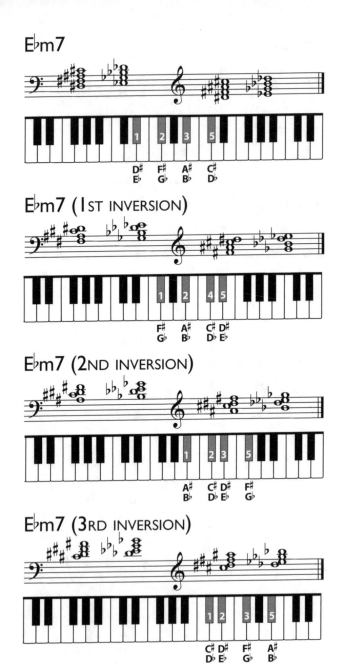

E♭m7 (1ST INVERSION)

E♭m7 (2ND INVERSION)

E♭m7 (3RD INVERSION)

D#
E♭

E♭m7(♭5)

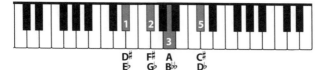

D#
Eb
Gb
A
Bbb
C#
Db

E♭m7(♭5) (1ST INVERSION)

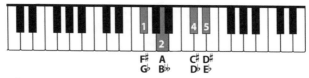

E♭m7(♭5) (2ND INVERSION)

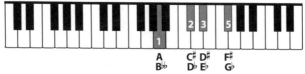

E♭m7(♭5) (3RD INVERSION)

E♭°7

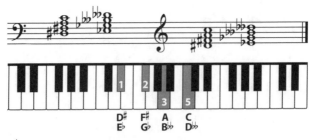

D♯ / E♭ | D♯/E♭ F♯/G♭ A/B♭♭ C/D♭♭

E♭°7 (1st INVERSION)

F♯/G♭ A/B♭♭ C/D♭♭ D♯/E♭

E♭°7 (2nd INVERSION)

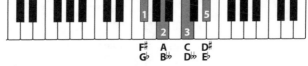

A/B♭♭ C/D♭♭ D♯/E♭ F♯/G♭

E♭°7 (3rd INVERSION)

C/D♭♭ D♯/E♭ F♯/G♭ A/B♭♭

E♭(add9)*

D♯ E♯ F× A♯
E♭ F G   B♭

E♭(add9)* (1ST INVERSION)

F× A♯   D♯ E♯
G   B♭   E♭ F

E♭(add9)* (2ND INVERSION)

A♯   D♯ E♯ F×
B♭   E♭ F G

E♭(add9)* (3RD INVERSION)

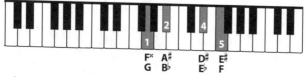

E♯ F× A♯   D♯
F G   B♭   E♭

* Sometimes called (add2)

E♭9

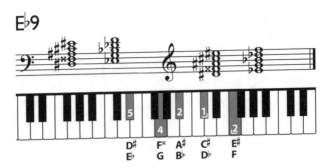

E♭maj9

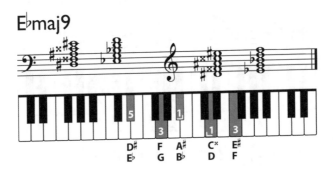

E♭m9

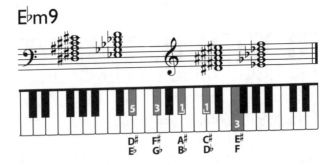

E♭maj7(♭5)

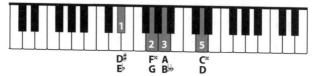

E♭maj7(♯5)

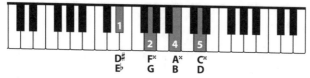

E♭7(♭5)

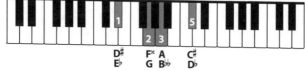

E♭7(♯5)

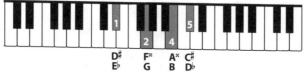

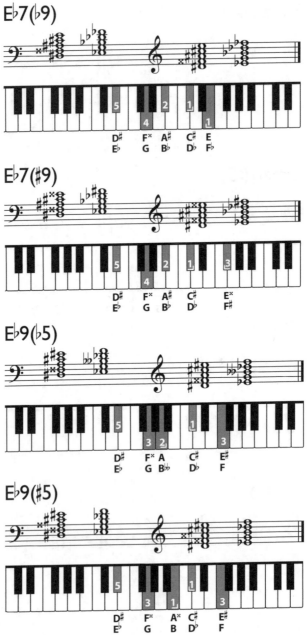

E

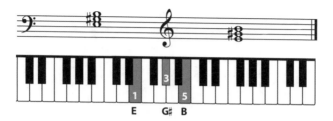

E   G♯   B

E (1ST INVERSION)

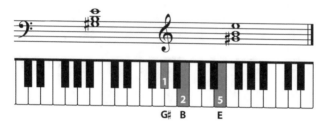

G♯   B   E

E (2ND INVERSION)

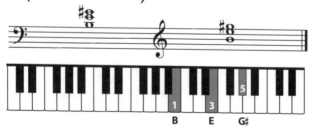

B   E   G♯

Em

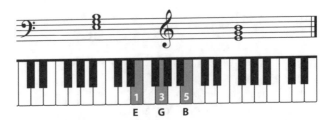

Em (1ST INVERSION)

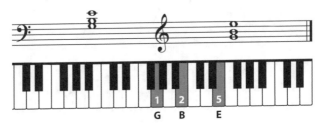

Em (2ND INVERSION)

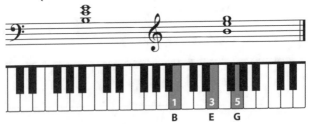

E

E°

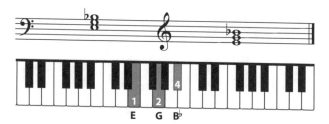

E G B♭

E° (1st inversion)

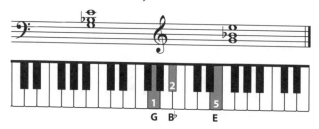

G B♭ E

E° (2nd inversion)

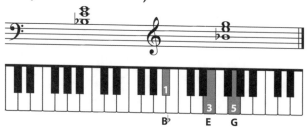

B♭ E G

E+

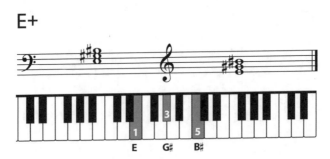

E   G♯   B♯

E+ (1ST INVERSION)

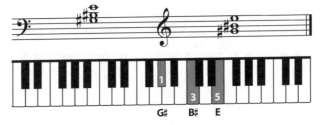

G♯   B♯   E

E+ (2ND INVERSION)

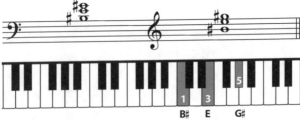

B♯   E   G♯

Esus2

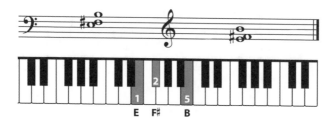

E   F#   B

Esus4

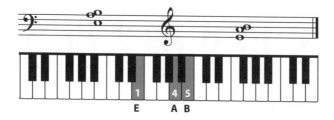

E   A B

E5 (POWER CHORD)

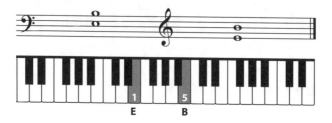

E   B

E

E6

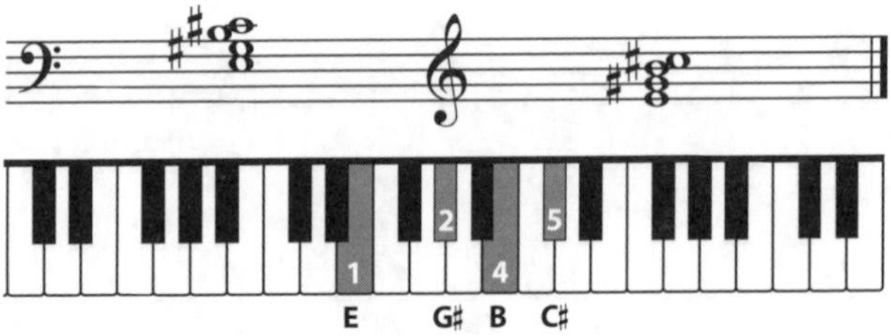

E G# B C#

E6 (1ST INVERSION)

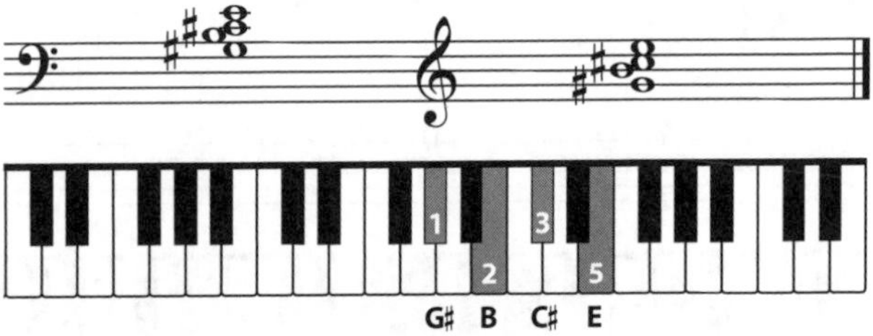

G# B C# E

E6 (2ND INVERSION)

B C# E G#

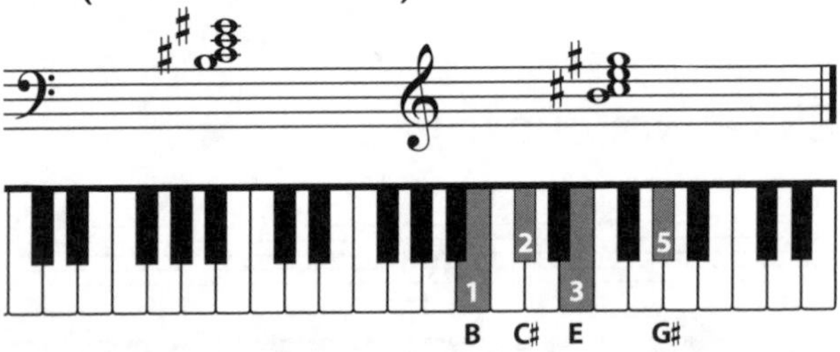

E6 (3RD INVERSION)

C# E G# B

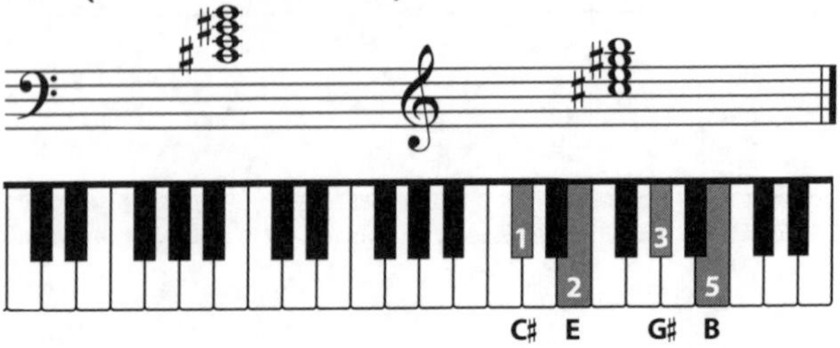

Em6

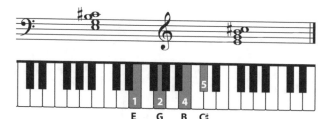

E G B C♯

Em6 (1ST INVERSION)

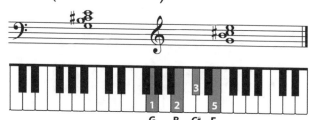

G B C♯ E

Em6 (2ND INVERSION)

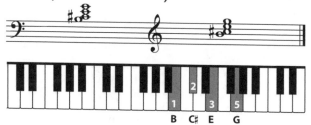

B C♯ E G

Em6 (3RD INVERSION)

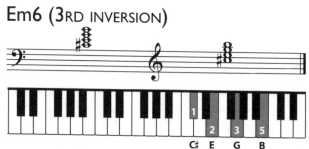

C♯ E G B

E7

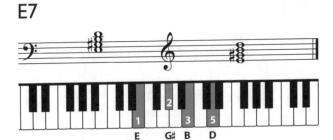

E · G# · B · D

E7 (1ST INVERSION)

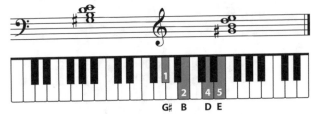

G# · B · D · E

E7 (2ND INVERSION)

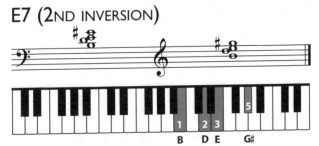

B · D · E · G#

E7 (3RD INVERSION)

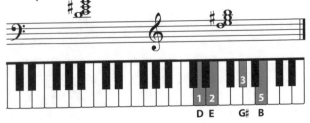

D · E · G# · B

Emaj7

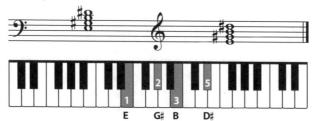

E G# B D#

Emaj7 (1ST INVERSION)

G# B D# E

Emaj7 (2ND INVERSION)

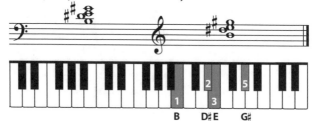

B D# E G#

Emaj7 (3RD INVERSION)

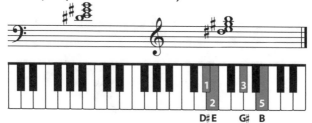

D# E G# B

E

Em7

Em7 (1ST INVERSION)

Em7 (2ND INVERSION)

Em7 (3RD INVERSION)

Em7(♭5)

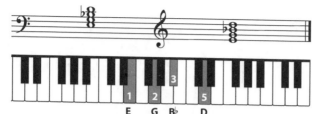

E G B♭ D

Em7(♭5) (1ST INVERSION)

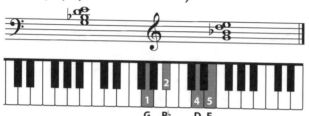

G B♭ D E

Em7(♭5) (2ND INVERSION)

B♭ D E G

Em7(♭5) (3RD INVERSION)

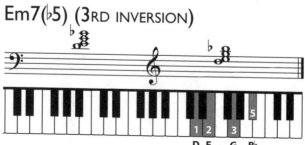

D E G B♭

E

E°7

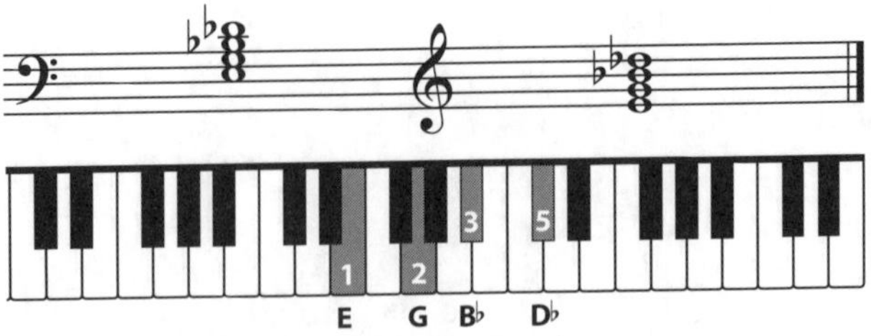

E   G   B♭   D♭

E°7 (1st INVERSION)

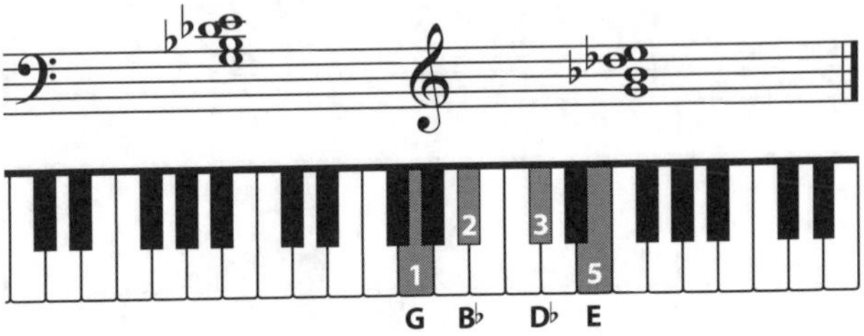

G   B♭   D♭   E

E°7 (2nd INVERSION)

B♭   D♭   E   G

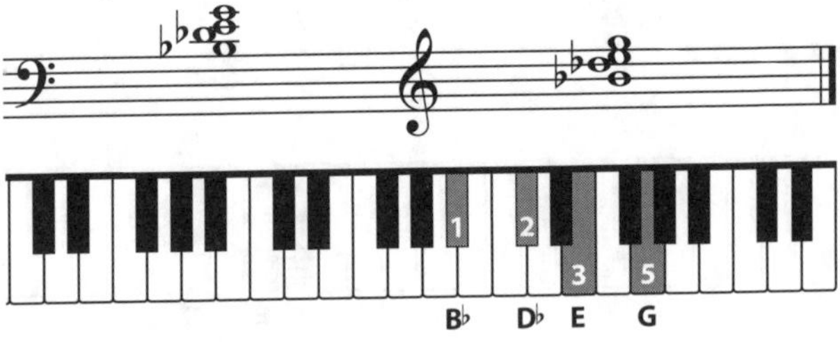

E°7 (3rd INVERSION)

D♭   E   G   B♭

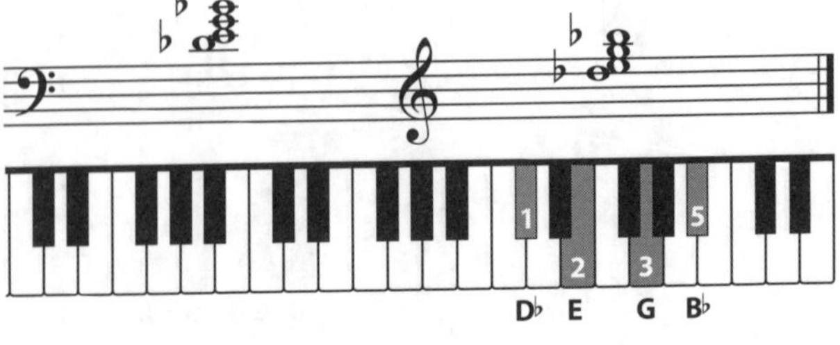

E(add9)*

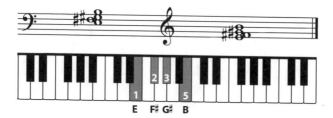

E F# G# B

E(add9)* (1ST INVERSION)

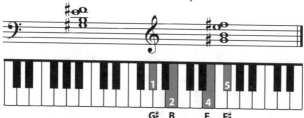

G# B E F#

E(add9)* (2ND INVERSION)

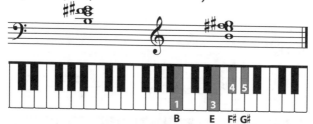

B E F# G#

E(add9)* (3RD INVERSION)

F# G# B E

E

* Sometimes called (add2)

E9

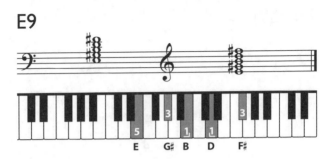

Emaj9

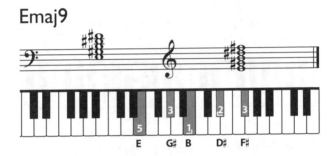

Em9

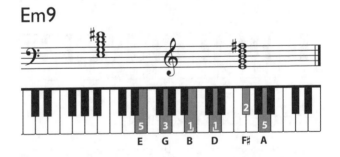

Emaj7(♭5)

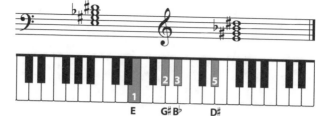

Emaj7(♯5)

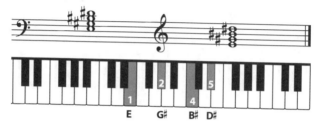

E7(♭5)

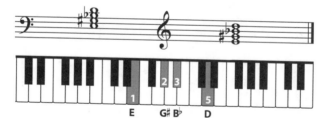

E7(♯5)

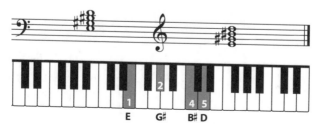

E7(♭9)

E7(♯9)

E

E9(♭5)

E9(♯5)

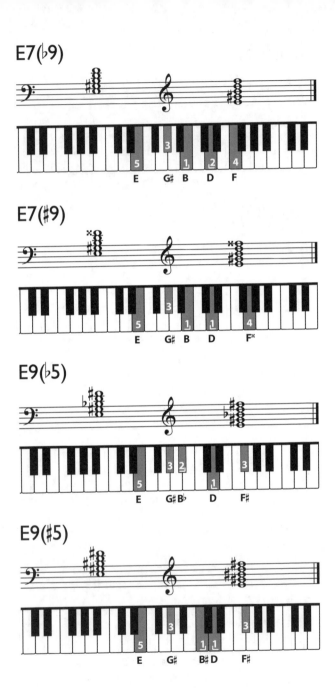

F

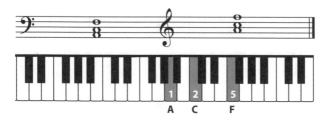

F (1ST INVERSION)

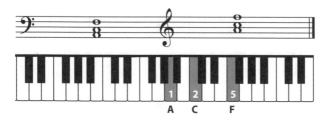

F (2ND INVERSION)

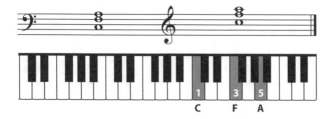

F

Fm

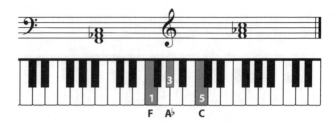

Fm (1ST INVERSION)

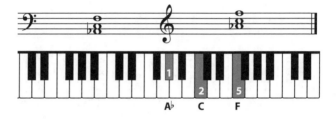

Fm (2ND INVERSION)

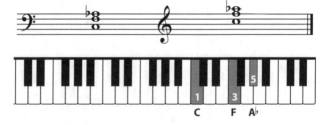

F

122

F°

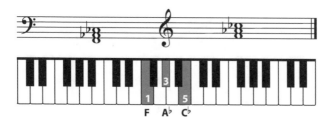

F° (1ST INVERSION)

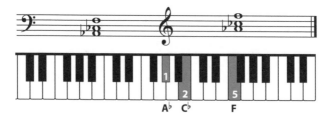

F

F° (2ND INVERSION)

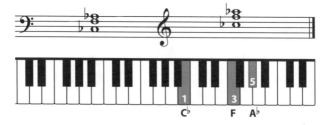

123

F+

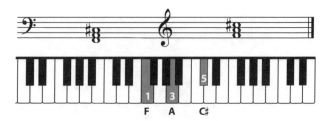

F+ (1ST INVERSION)

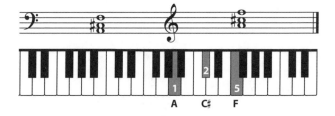

F+ (2ND INVERSION)

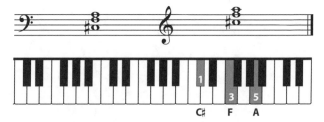

F

Fsus2

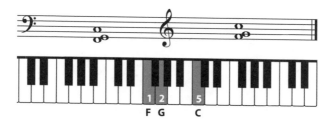

Fsus4

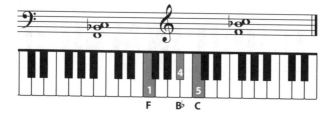

F5 (POWER CHORD)

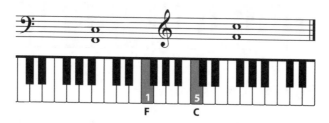

F

F6

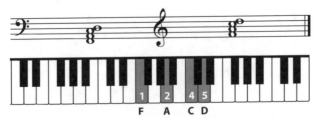

F A C D

F6 (1ST INVERSION)

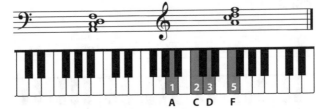

A C D F

F6 (2ND INVERSION)

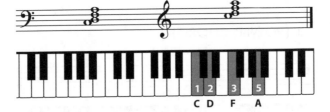

C D F A

F6 (3RD INVERSION)

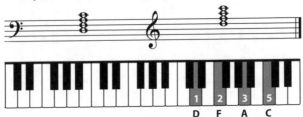

D F A C

F

Fm6

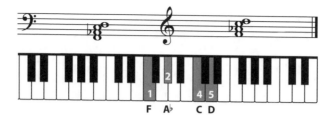

Fm6 (1ST INVERSION)

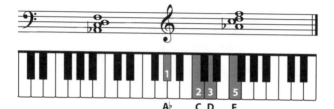

Fm6 (2ND INVERSION)

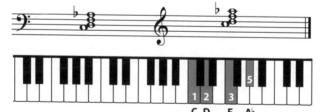

Fm6 (3RD INVERSION)

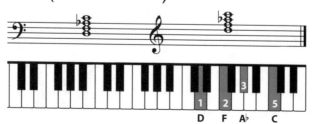

F

127

F7

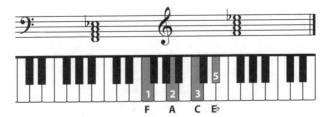

F7 (1ST INVERSION)

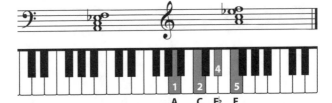

F7 (2ND INVERSION)

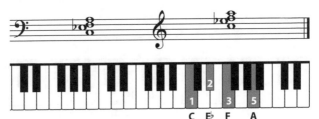

F7 (3RD INVERSION)

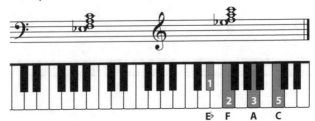

F

Fmaj7

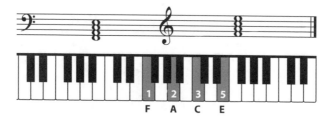

F A C E

Fmaj7 (1ST INVERSION)

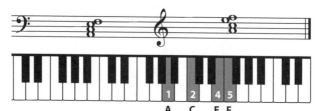

A C E F

F

Fmaj7 (2ND INVERSION)

C E F A

Fmaj7 (3RD INVERSION)

E F A C

Fm7

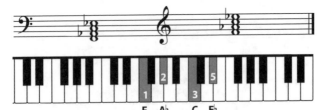

F A♭ C E♭

Fm7 (1ST INVERSION)

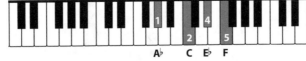

A♭ C E♭ F

Fm7 (2ND INVERSION)

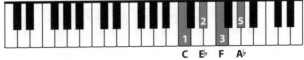

C E♭ F A♭

Fm7 (3RD INVERSION)

E♭ F A♭ C

Fm7(♭5)

F A♭ C♭ E♭

Fm7(♭5) (1ST INVERSION)

A♭ C♭ E♭ F

Fm7(♭5) (2ND INVERSION)

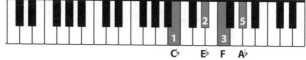

C♭ E♭ F A♭

Fm7(♭5) (3RD INVERSION)

E♭ F A♭ C♭

F

F°7

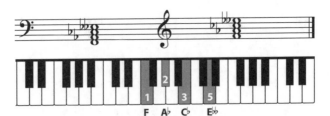

F A♭ C♭ E♭♭

F°7 (1ST INVERSION)

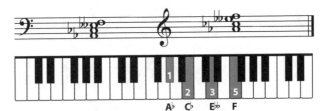

A♭ C♭ E♭♭ F

F°7 (2ND INVERSION)

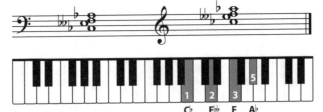

C♭ E♭♭ F A♭

F°7 (3RD INVERSION)

E♭♭ F A♭ C♭

F(add9)*

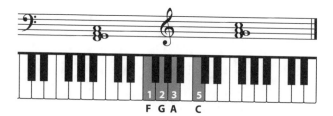

F G A C

F(add9)* (1ST INVERSION)

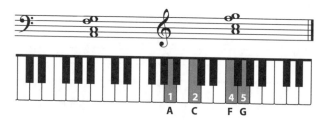

A C F G

F(add9)* (2ND INVERSION)

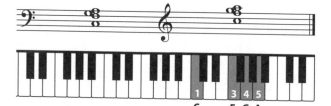

C F G A

F(add9)* (3RD INVERSION)

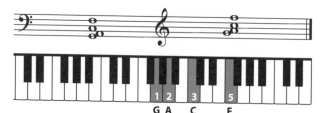

G A C F

F

133

F9

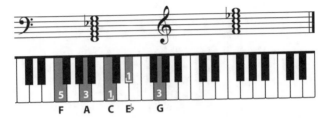

F A C E♭ G

Fmaj9

F A C E G

Fm9

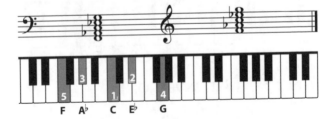

F A♭ C E♭ G

F

134

Fmaj7(♭5)

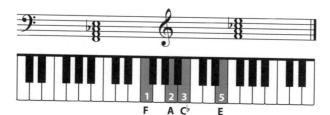

Fmaj7(♯5)

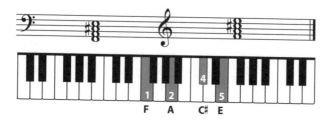

F7(♭5)

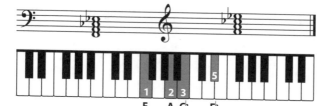

F7(♯5)

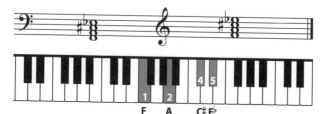

F

F7(♭9)

F7(♯9)

F9(♭5)

F9(♯5)

F

F#

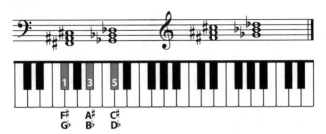

F#　A#　C#
G♭　B♭　D♭

F# (1st inversion)

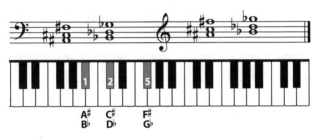

A#　C#　F#
B♭　D♭　G♭

F# (2nd inversion)

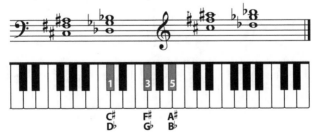

C#　F#　A#
D♭　G♭　B♭

F#m

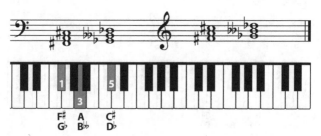

F#m (1ST INVERSION)

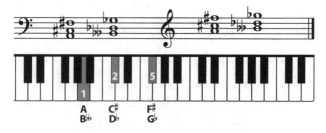

F#m (2ND INVERSION)

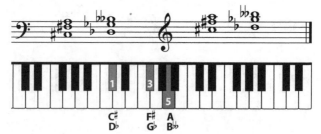

F#
Gb

138

F#°

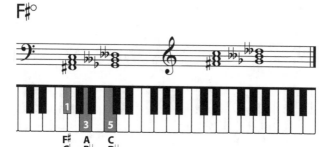

F#° (1ST INVERSION)

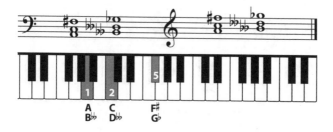

F#° (2ND INVERSION)

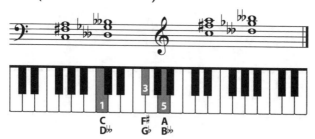

F#+

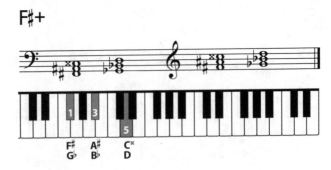

F#+ (1ST INVERSION)

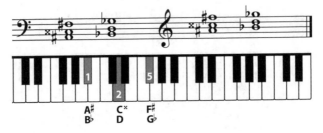

F#
Gb

F#+ (2ND INVERSION)

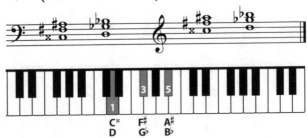

F#sus2

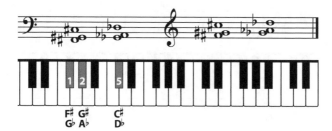

F#sus4

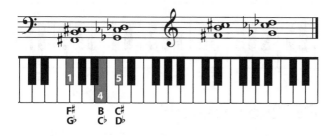

F#5 (POWER CHORD)

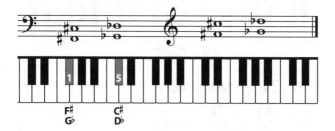

F#
Gb

141

F♯6

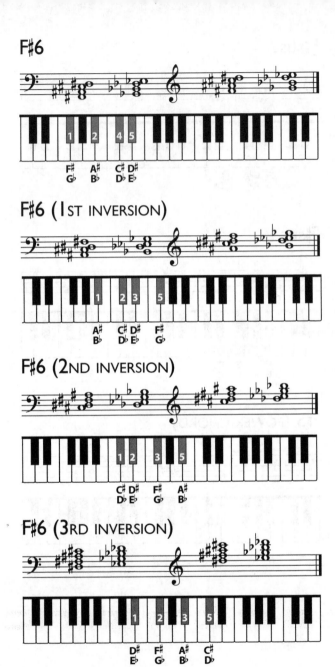

F♯6 (1ST INVERSION)

F♯6 (2ND INVERSION)

F♯
G♭

F♯6 (3RD INVERSION)

F#m6

F#m6 (1ST INVERSION)

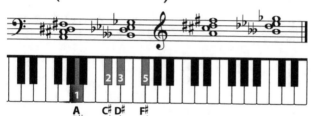

F#m6 (2ND INVERSION)

F#
Gb

F#m6 (3RD INVERSION)

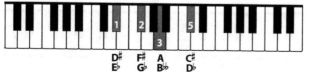

F#7

F#7 (1ST INVERSION)

F#
Gb

F#7 (2ND INVERSION)

F#7 (3RD INVERSION)

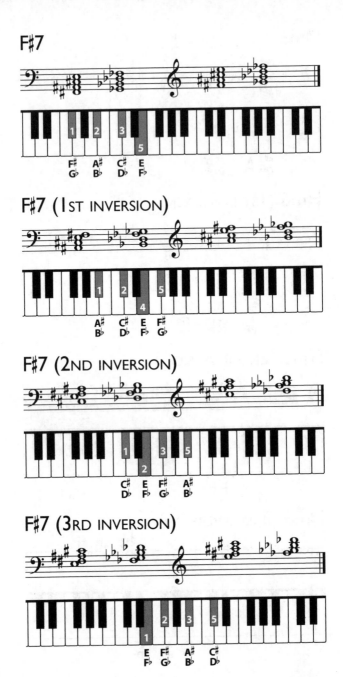

F#maj7

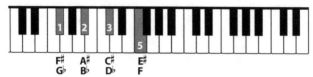

F#   A#   C#   E#
Gb   Bb   Db   F

F#maj7 (1ST INVERSION)

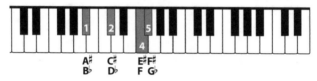

A#   C#   E#F#
Bb   Db   F Gb

F#maj7 (2ND INVERSION)

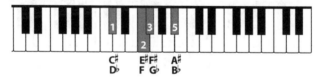

C#   E#F#   A#
Db   F Gb   Bb

F#maj7 (3RD INVERSION)

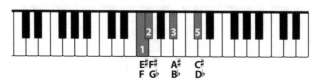

E#F#   A#   C#
F Gb   Bb   Db

F#
Gb

F#m7

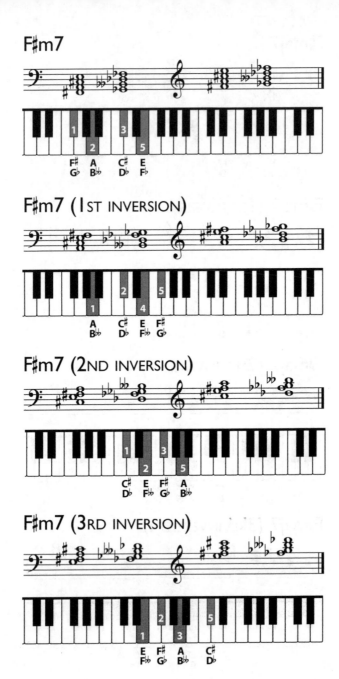

F#m7 (1ST INVERSION)

F#m7 (2ND INVERSION)

F#m7 (3RD INVERSION)

F#
Gb

F#m7(♭5)

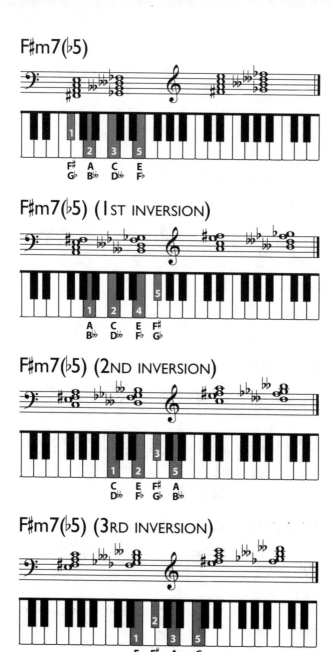

F#m7(♭5) (1ST INVERSION)

F#m7(♭5) (2ND INVERSION)

F#m7(♭5) (3RD INVERSION)

F#
G♭

F#°7

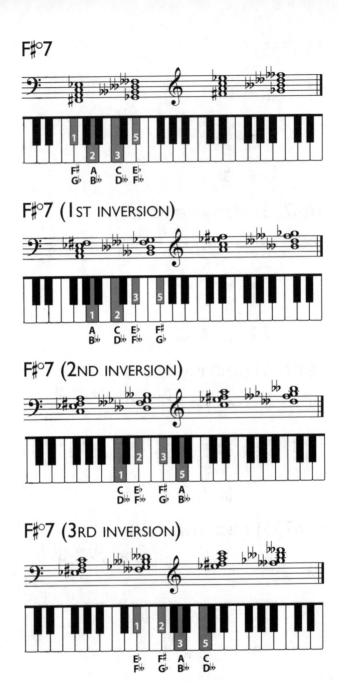

F#°7 (1ST INVERSION)

F#°7 (2ND INVERSION)

F#
G♭

F#°7 (3RD INVERSION)

F#(add9)*

F# G#A# C#
G♭ A♭B♭ D♭

F#(add9)* (1ST INVERSION)

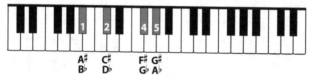

A# C# F# G#
B♭ D♭ G♭ A♭

F#(add9)* (2ND INVERSION)

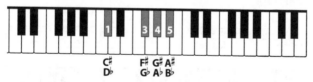

C# F# G#A#
D♭ G♭ A♭B♭

F#(add9)* (3RD INVERSION)

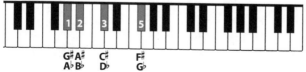

G#A# C# F#
A♭B♭ D♭ G♭

F#
G♭

Sometimes called (add2)

149

F#9

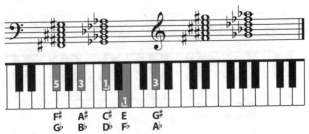

F#maj9

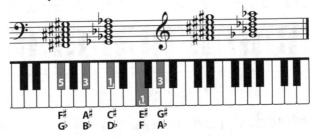

F#m9

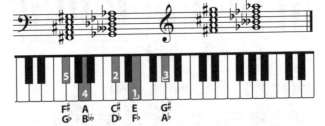

F#maj7(♭5)

F#maj7(#5)

F#7(♭5)

F#7(#5)

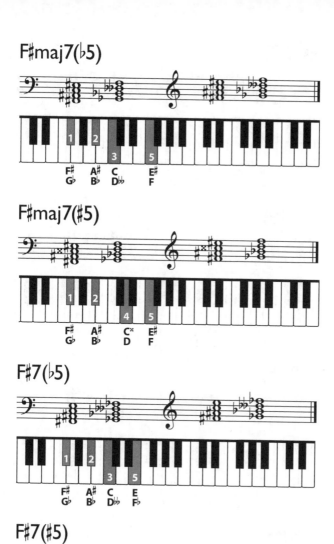

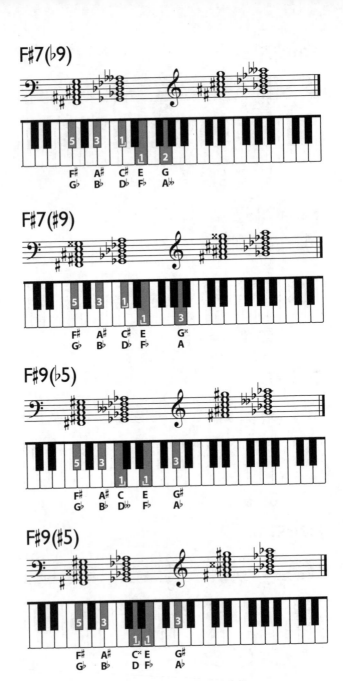

G

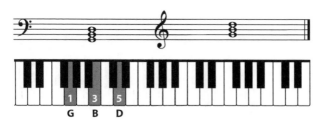

G (1ST INVERSION)

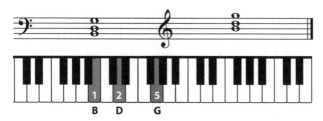

G (2ND INVERSION)

G

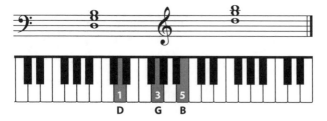

Gm

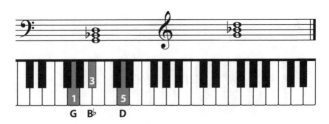

Gm (1ST INVERSION)

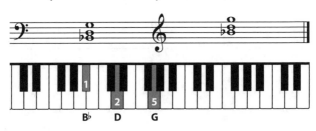

Gm (2ND INVERSION)

G

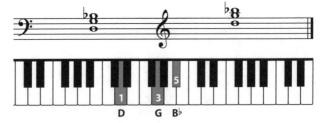

G°

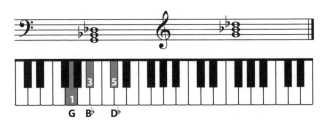

G° (1ST INVERSION)

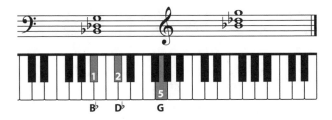

G° (2ND INVERSION)

G

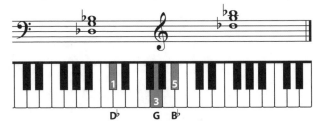

G+

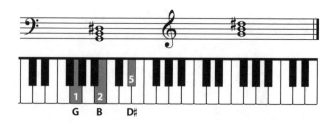

G+ (1ST INVERSION)

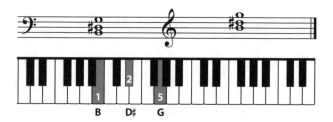

G+ (2ND INVERSION)

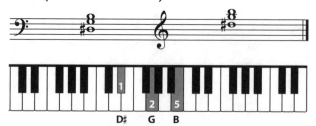

Gsus2

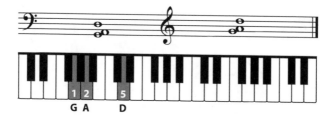

Gsus4

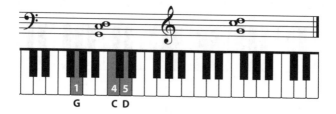

G5 (POWER CHORD)

G

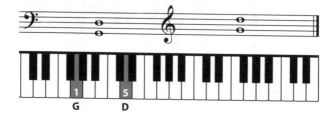

G6

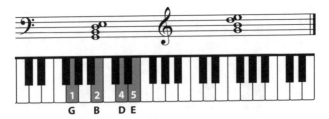

G B D E

G6 (1ST INVERSION)

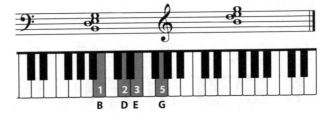

B D E G

G6 (2ND INVERSION)

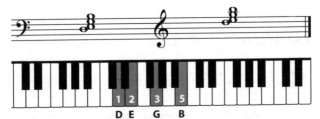

D E G B

G6 (3RD INVERSION)

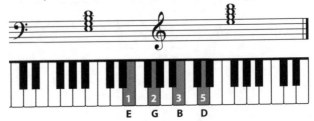

E G B D

G

Gm6

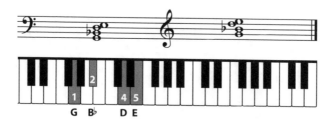

G B♭ D E

Gm6 (1ST INVERSION)

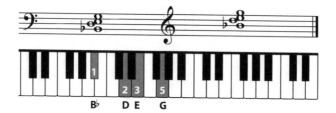

B♭ D E G

Gm6 (2ND INVERSION)

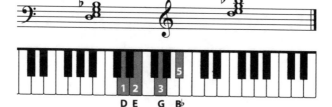

D E G B♭

G

Gm6 (3RD INVERSION)

E G B♭ D

G7

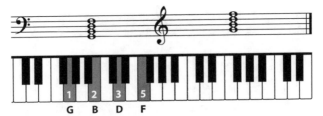

G B D F

G7 (1ST INVERSION)

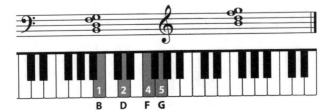

B D F G

G7 (2ND INVERSION)

G

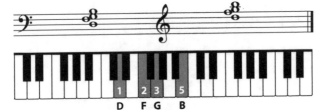

D F G B

G7 (3RD INVERSION)

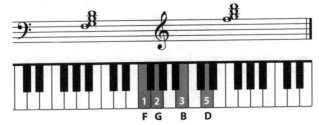

F G B D

Gmaj7

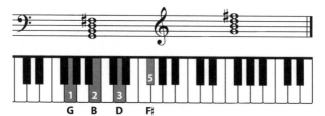

G B D F#

Gmaj7 (1ST INVERSION)

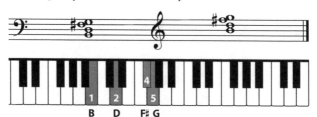

B D F# G

Gmaj7 (2ND INVERSION)

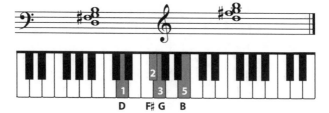

D F# G B

G

Gmaj7 (3RD INVERSION)

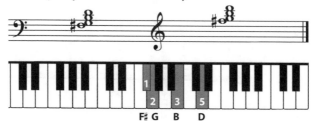

F# G B D

Gm7

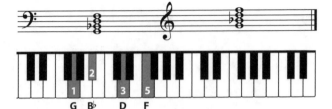

G B♭ D F

Gm7 (1ST INVERSION)

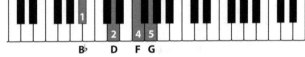

B♭ D F G

Gm7 (2ND INVERSION)

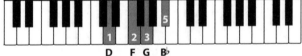

D F G B♭

Gm7 (3RD INVERSION)

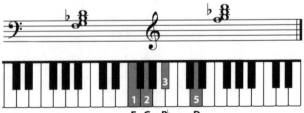

F G B♭ D

Gm7(♭5)

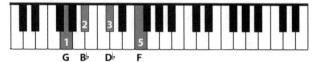

G B♭ D♭ F

Gm7(♭5) (1ST INVERSION)

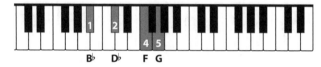

B♭ D♭ F G

Gm7(♭5) (2ND INVERSION)

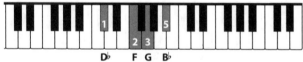

D♭ F G B♭

G

Gm7(♭5) (3RD INVERSION)

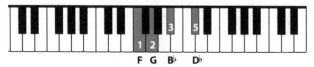

F G B♭ D♭

G°7

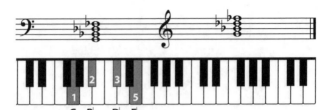

G B♭ D♭ F♭

G°7 (1ST INVERSION)

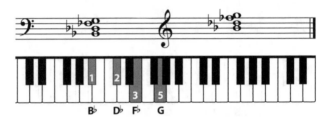

B♭ D♭ F♭ G

G°7 (2ND INVERSION)

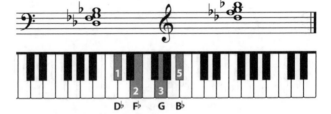

D♭ F♭ G B♭

G°7 (3RD INVERSION)

F♭ G B♭ D♭

G(add9)*

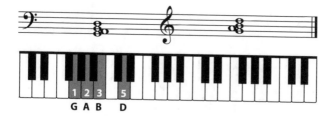

1 2 3 5
G A B D

G(add9)* (1ST INVERSION)

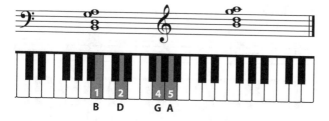

1 2 4 5
B D G A

G(add9)* (2ND INVERSION)

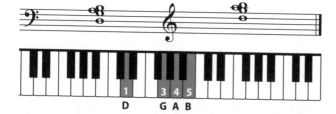

1 3 4 5
D G A B

G(add9)* (3RD INVERSION)

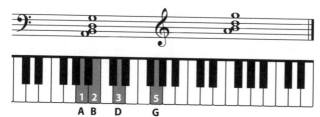

1 2 3 5
A B D G

G

Sometimes called (add2)

165

G9

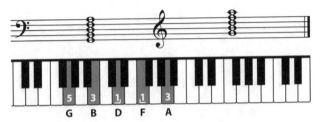

G B D F A

Gmaj9

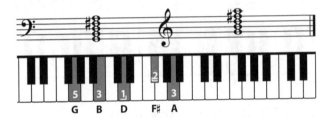

G B D F# A

Gm9

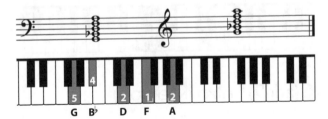

G B♭ D F A

Gmaj7(♭5)

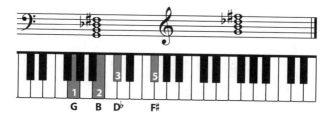

Gmaj7(♯5)

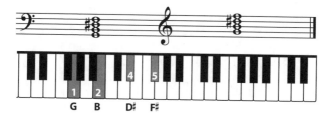

G7(♭5)

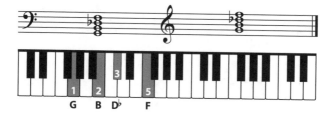

G

G7(♯5)

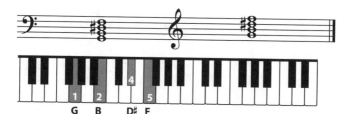

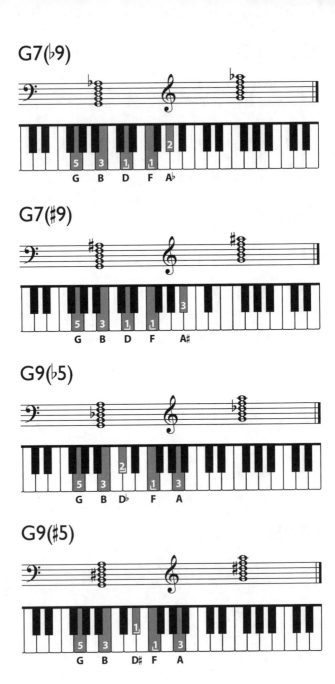

A♭

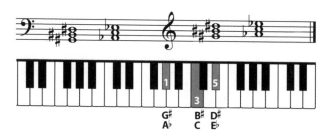

G♯ / A♭ B♯ / C D♯ / E♭

A♭ (1ST INVERSION)

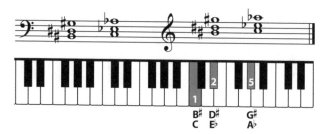

B♯ / C D♯ / E♭ G♯ / A♭

A♭ (2ND INVERSION)

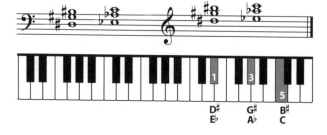

D♯ / E♭ G♯ / A♭ B♯ / C

A♭m

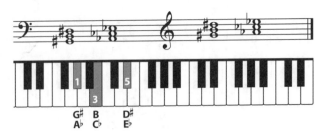

G♯   B   D♯
A♭   C♭ E♭

A♭m (1ST INVERSION)

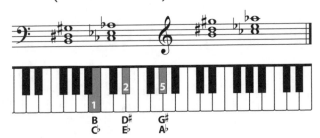

B   D♯   G♯
C♭ E♭   A♭

A♭m (2ND INVERSION)

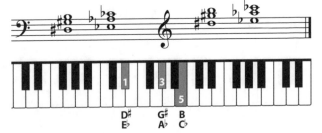

D♯   G♯   B
E♭   A♭   C♭

A♭°

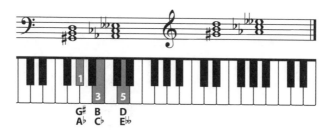

G# B   D
A♭ C♭ E♭♭

A♭° (1st inversion)

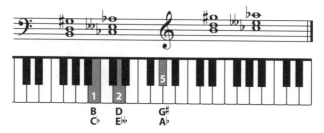

B   D   G#
C♭ E♭♭ A♭

A♭° (2nd inversion)

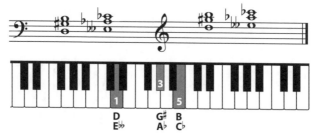

D   G# B
E♭♭   A♭ C♭

G#
A♭

A♭+

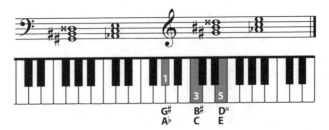

G♯ B♯ D×
A♭ C   E

A♭+ (1ST INVERSION)

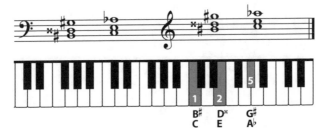

B♯ D× G♯
C   E   A♭

A♭+ (2ND INVERSION)

G♯
A♭

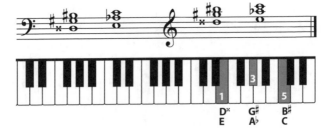

D× G♯ B♯
E   A♭ C

A♭sus2

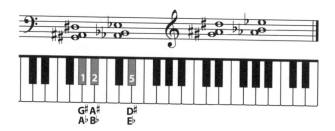

A♭sus4

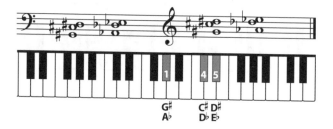

A♭5 (POWER CHORD)

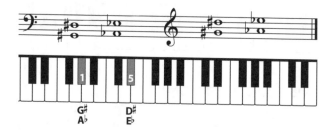

A♭6

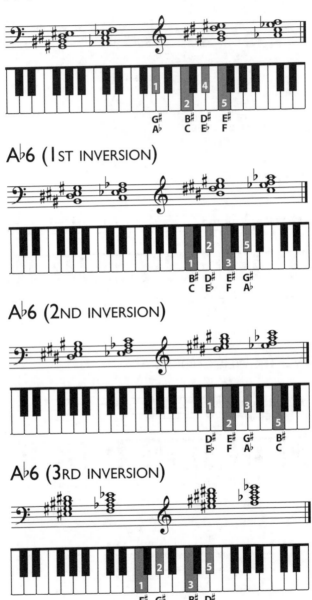

A♭6 (1ST INVERSION)

A♭6 (2ND INVERSION)

A♭6 (3RD INVERSION)

G♯
A♭

A♭m6

G♯ | B | D♯ | E♯
A♭ | C♭ | E♭ | F

A♭m6 (1ST INVERSION)

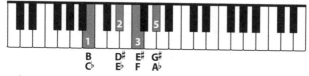

B | D♯ | E♯ | G♯
C♭ | E♭ | F | A♭

A♭m6 (2ND INVERSION)

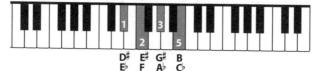

D♯ | E♯ | G♯ | B
E♭ | F | A♭ | C♭

A♭m6 (3RD INVERSION)

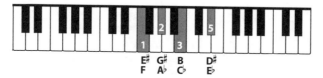

E♯ | G♯ | B | D♯
F | A♭ | C♭ | E♭

A♭7

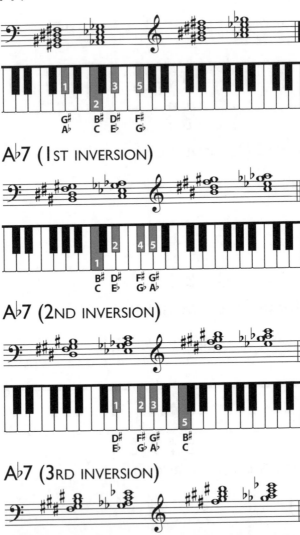

A♭7 (1ST INVERSION)

A♭7 (2ND INVERSION)

G#
A♭

A♭7 (3RD INVERSION)

A♭maj7

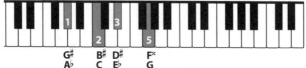

G♯   B♯ D♯   F×
A♭   C   E♭   G

A♭maj7 (1ST INVERSION)

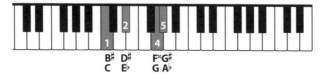

B♯ D♯   F× G♯
C   E♭   G A♭

A♭maj7 (2ND INVERSION)

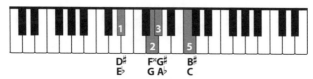

D♯   F×G♯   B♯
E♭   G A♭   C

G♯
A♭

A♭maj7 (3RD INVERSION)

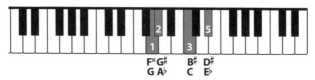

F×G♯   B♯ D♯
G A♭   C   E♭

A♭m7

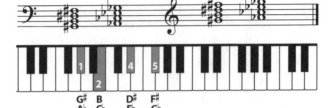

G♯ B D♯ F♯
A♭ C♭ E♭ G♭

A♭m7 (1st inversion)

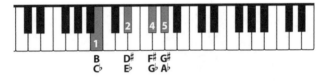

B D♯ F♯ G♯
C♭ E♭ G♭ A♭

A♭m7 (2nd inversion)

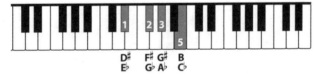

D♯ F♯ G♯ B
E♭ G♭ A♭ C♭

A♭m7 (3rd inversion)

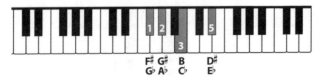

F♯ G♯ B D♯
G♭ A♭ C♭ E♭

G♯
A♭

178

A♭m7(♭5)

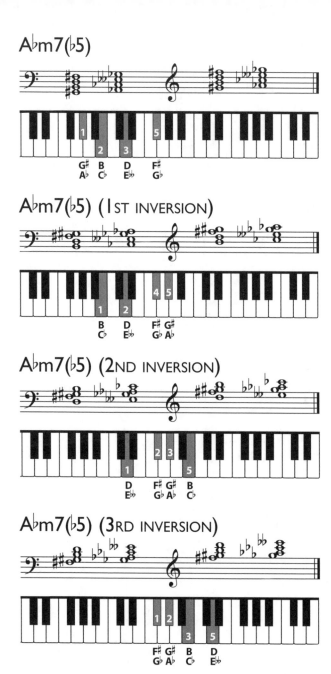

A♭m7(♭5) (1ST INVERSION)

A♭m7(♭5) (2ND INVERSION)

A♭m7(♭5) (3RD INVERSION)

G#
A♭

A♭°7

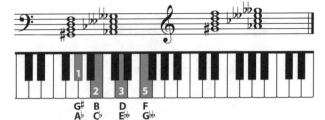

G♯ B D F
A♭ C♭ E♭♭ G♭♭

A♭°7 (1ST INVERSION)

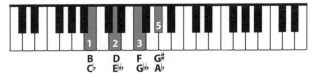

B D F G♯
C♭ E♭♭ G♭♭ A♭

A♭°7 (2ND INVERSION)

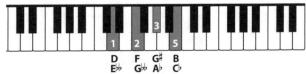

D F G♯ B
E♭♭ G♭♭ A♭ C♭

A♭°7 (3RD INVERSION)

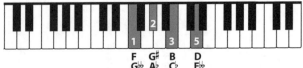

F G♯ B D
G♭♭ A♭ C♭ E♭♭

A♭(add9)*

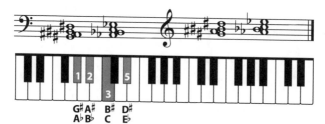

A♭(add9)* (1ST INVERSION)

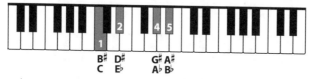

A♭(add9)* (2ND INVERSION)

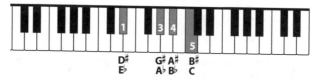

G#
A♭

A♭(add9)* (3RD INVERSION)

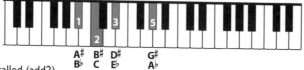

*Sometimes called (add2)

A♭9

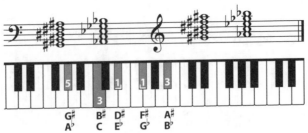

G♯ B♯ D♯ F♯ A♯
A♭ C E♭ G♭ B♭

A♭maj9

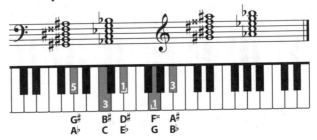

G♯ B♯ D♯ F× A♯
A♭ C E♭ G B♭

A♭m9

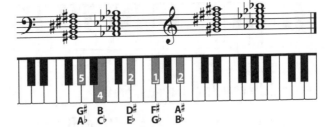

G♯ B D♯ F♯ A♯
A♭ C♭ E♭ G♭ B♭

A♭maj7(♭5)

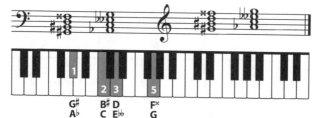

G♯/A♭ B♯/C D/E♭♭ F×/G

A♭maj7(♯5)

G♯/A♭ B♯/C D×/E F×/G

A♭7(♭5)

G♯/A♭ B♯/C D/E♭♭ F♯/G♭

G♯
A♭

A♭7(♯5)

G♯/A♭ B♯/C D×/E F♯/G♭

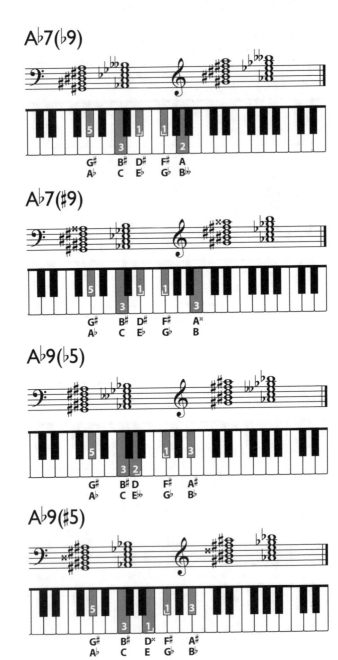

A

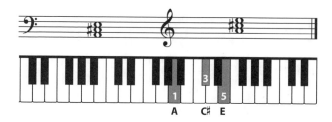

A   C#   E

A (1ST INVERSION)

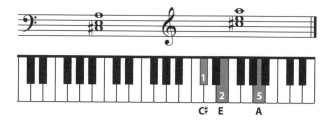

C#   E   A

A (2ND INVERSION)

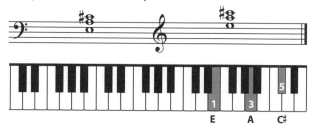

E   A   C#

Am

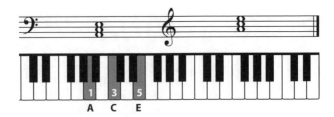

Am (1ST INVERSION)

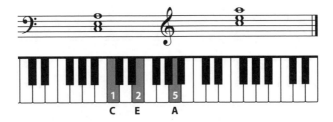

Am (2ND INVERSION)

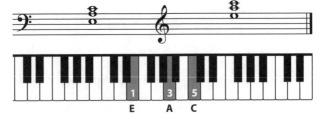

186

A°

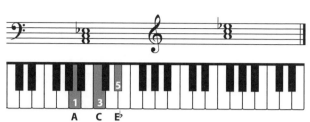

A   C   E♭

A° (1ST INVERSION)

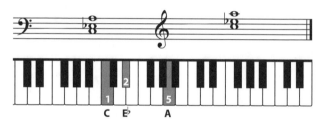

C   E♭   A

A° (2ND INVERSION)

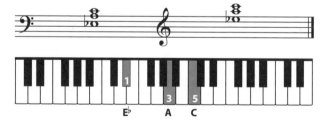

E♭   A   C

A

A+

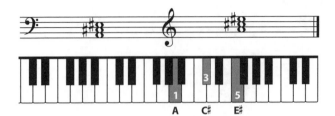

A+ (1st inversion)

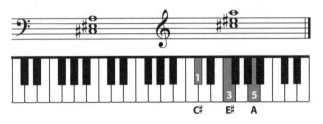

A+ (2nd inversion)

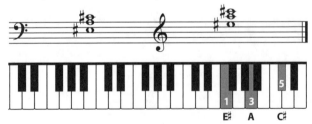

A

Asus2

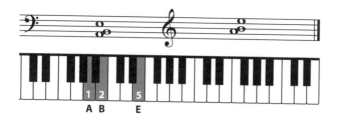

Asus4

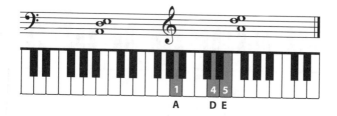

A5 (POWER CHORD)

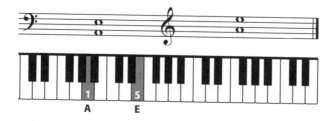

A

189

A6

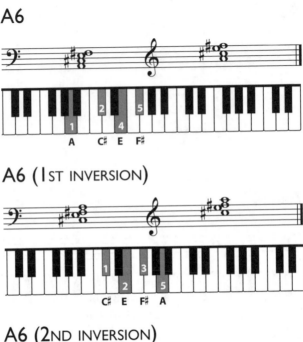

A   C♯   E   F♯

A6 (1ST INVERSION)

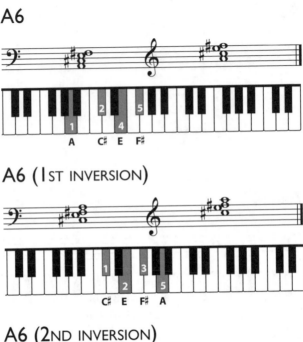

C♯   E   F♯   A

A6 (2ND INVERSION)

E   F♯   A   C♯

A6 (3RD INVERSION)

F♯   A   C♯   E

A

Am6

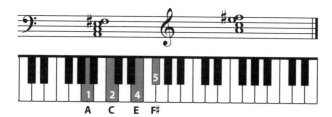

A C E F#

Am6 (1ST INVERSION)

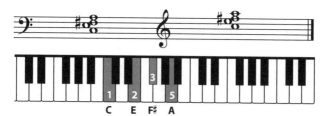

C E F# A

Am6 (2ND INVERSION)

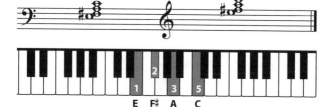

E F# A C

Am6 (3RD INVERSION)

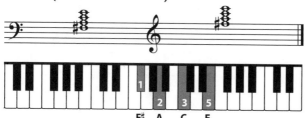

F# A C E

A

A7

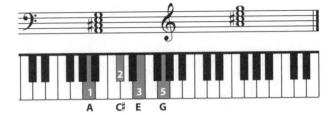

A   C♯   E   G

A7 (1st inversion)

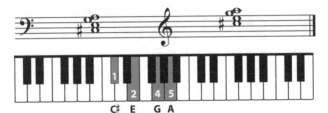

C♯   E   G   A

A7 (2nd inversion)

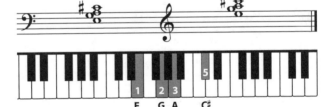

E   G   A   C♯

A7 (3rd inversion)

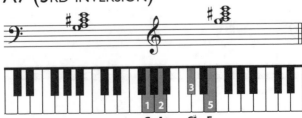

G   A   C♯   E

A

Amaj7

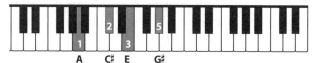

A C# E G#

Amaj7 (1ST INVERSION)

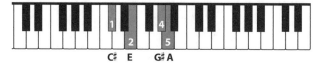

C# E G# A

Amaj7 (2ND INVERSION)

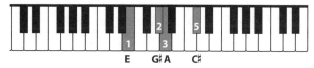

E G# A C#

Amaj7 (3RD INVERSION)

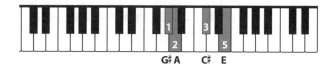

G# A C# E

Am7

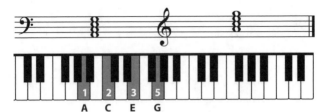

A C E G

Am7 (1ST INVERSION)

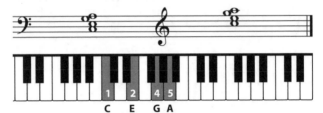

C E G A

Am7 (2ND INVERSION)

E G A C

Am7 (3RD INVERSION)

G A C E

A

Am7(♭5)

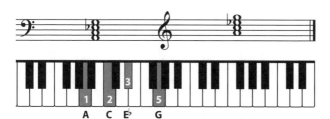

A   C   E♭   G

Am7(♭5) (1ST INVERSION)

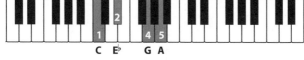

C   E♭   G   A

Am7(♭5) (2ND INVERSION)

E♭   G   A   C

Am7(♭5) (3RD INVERSION)

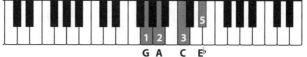

G   A   C   E♭

A

A°7

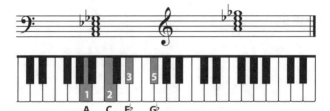

A°7 (1ST INVERSION)

A°7 (2ND INVERSION)

A°7 (3RD INVERSION)

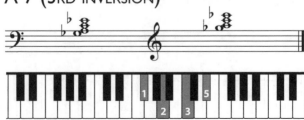

A

A(add9)*

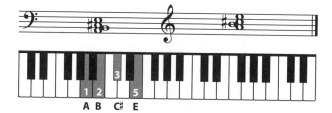

A B C♯ E

A(add9)* (1ST INVERSION)

C♯ E A B

A(add9)* (2ND INVERSION)

E A B C♯

A(add9)* (3RD INVERSION)

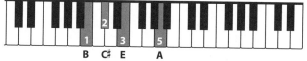

B C♯ E A

*ometimes called (add2)

A9

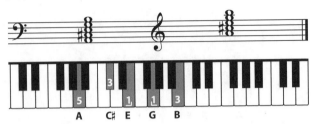

Amaj9

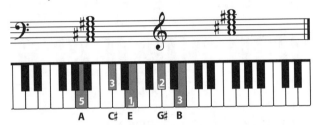

Am9

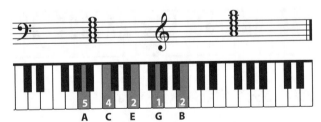

A

Amaj7(♭5)

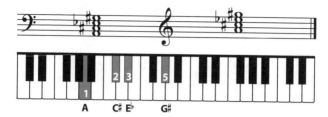

Amaj7(♯5)

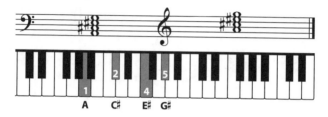

A7(♭5)

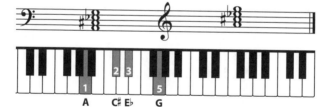

A7(♯5)

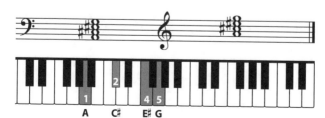

A7(♭9)

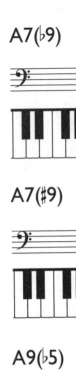

A C# E G B♭

A7(#9)

A C# E G B#

A9(♭5)

A C# E♭ G B

A9(#5)

A C# E# G B

B♭

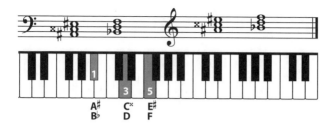

B♭ (1ST INVERSION)

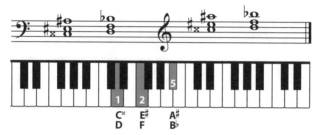

B♭ (2ND INVERSION)

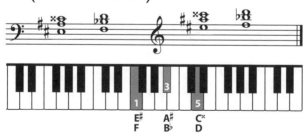

A♯
B♭

B♭m

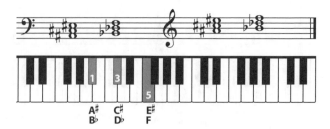

A♯ C♯ E♯
B♭ D♭ F

B♭m (1ST INVERSION)

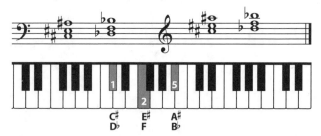

C♯ E♯ A♯
D♭ F B♭

B♭m (2ND INVERSION)

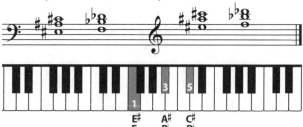

E♯ A♯ C♯
F B♭ D♭

A♯
B♭

B♭°

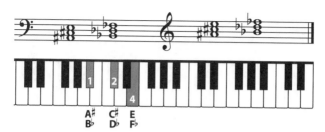

B♭° (1ST INVERSION)

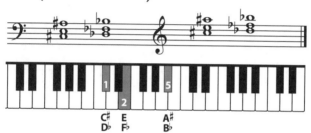

B♭° (2ND INVERSION)

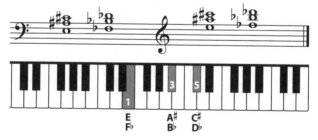

A♯
B♭

B♭+

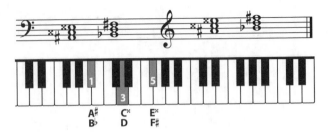

A♯
B♭   C×
D   E×
F♯

B♭+ (1ST INVERSION)

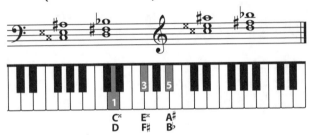

C×
D   E×
F♯   A♯
B♭

B♭+ (2ND INVERSION)

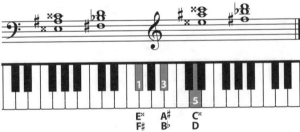

E×
F♯   A♯
B♭   C×
D

A♯
B♭

B♭sus2

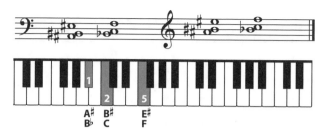

A♯ B♯ E♯
B♭ C F

B♭sus4

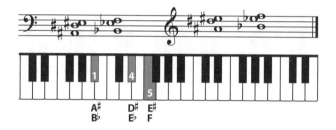

A♯ D♯ E♯
B♭ E♭ F

B♭5 (POWER CHORD)

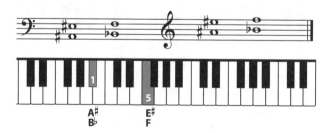

A♯ E♯
B♭ F

B♭6

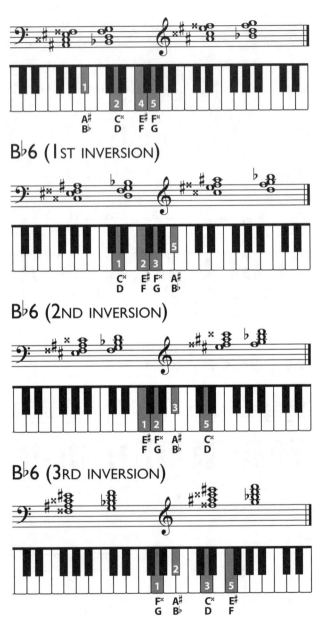

B♭6 (1ST INVERSION)

B♭6 (2ND INVERSION)

B♭6 (3RD INVERSION)

A♯
B♭

B♭m6

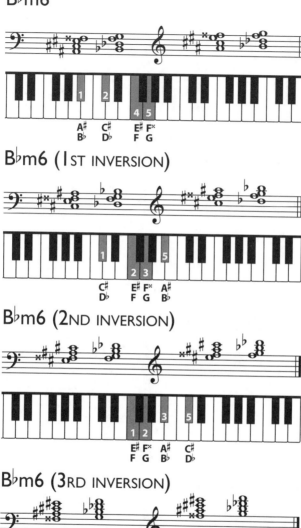

B♭m6 (1ST INVERSION)

B♭m6 (2ND INVERSION)

B♭m6 (3RD INVERSION)

A#
B♭

B♭7

A♯
B♭ / C× D / E♯ F / G♯ A♭

B♭7 (1st inversion)

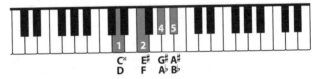

C× D / E♯ F / G♯ A♭ / A♯ B♭

B♭7 (2nd inversion)

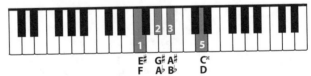

E♯ F / G♯ A♭ / A♯ B♭ / C× D

B♭7 (3rd inversion)

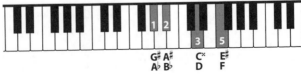

G♯ A♭ / A♯ B♭ / C× D / E♯ F

A♯
B♭

B♭maj7

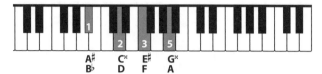

B♭maj7 (1ST INVERSION)

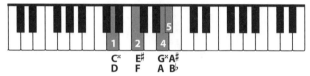

B♭maj7 (2ND INVERSION)

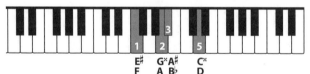

B♭maj7 (3RD INVERSION)

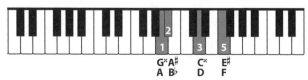

A#
B♭

B♭m7

A♯ C♯ E♯ G♯
B♭ D♭ F A♭

B♭m7 (1ST INVERSION)

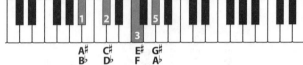

C♯ E♯ G♯ A♯
D♭ F A♭ B♭

B♭m7 (2ND INVERSION)

E♯ G♯ A♯ C♯
F A♭ B♭ D♭

B♭m7 (3RD INVERSION)

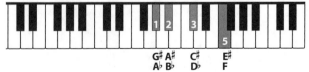

G♯ A♯ C♯ E♯
A♭ B♭ D♭ F

A♯
B♭

B♭m7(♭5)

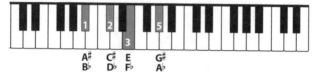

A♯ C♯ E G♯
B♭ D♭ F♭ A♭

B♭m7(♭5) (1ST INVERSION)

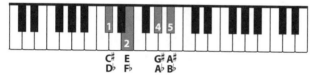

C♯ E G♯ A♯
D♭ F♭ A♭ B♭

B♭m7(♭5) (2ND INVERSION)

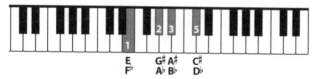

E G♯ A♯ C♯
F♭ A♭ B♭ D♭

B♭m7(♭5) (3RD INVERSION)

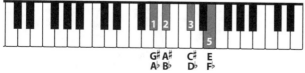

G♯ A♯ C♯ E
A♭ B♭ D♭ F♭

A♯
B♭

211

B♭°7

A♯ C♯ E G
B♭ D♭ F♭ A♭♭

B♭°7 (1ST INVERSION)

C♯ E G A♯
D♭ F♭ A♭♭ B♭

B♭°7 (2ND INVERSION)

E G A♯ C♯
F♭ A♭♭ B♭ D♭

B♭°7 (3RD INVERSION)

G A♯ C♯ E
A♭♭ B♭ D♭ F♭

A♯
B♭

B♭(add9)*

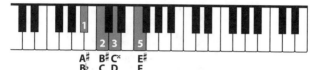

A♯ B♯ C× E♯
B♭ C D   F

B♭(add9)* (1ST INVERSION)

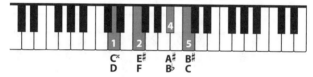

C× E♯ A♯ B♯
D   F   B♭ C

B♭(add9)* (2ND INVERSION)

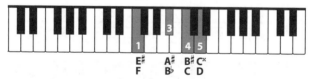

E♯ A♯ B♯ C×
F   B♭ C D

B♭(add9)* (3RD INVERSION)

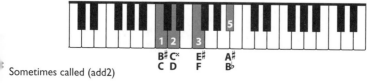

B♯ C× E♯ A♯
C D   F   B♭

A♯
B♭

Sometimes called (add2)

213

B♭9

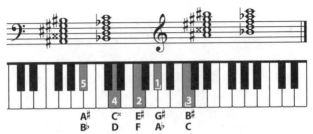

A♯	C×	E♯	G♯	B♯
B♭	D	F	A♭	C

B♭maj9

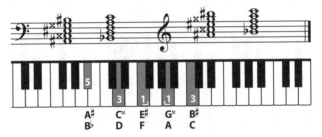

A♯	C×	E♯	G×	B♯
B♭	D	F	A	C

B♭m9

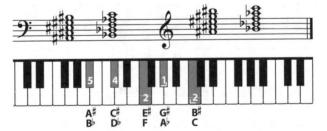

A♯	C♯	E♯	G♯	B♯
B♭	D♭	F	A♭	C

214

B♭maj7(♭5)

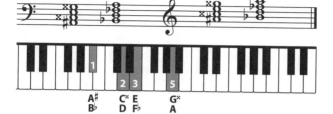

A♯   C×   E   G×
B♭   D   F♭   A

B♭maj7(♯5)

A♯   C×   E×   G×
B♭   D   F♯   A

B♭7(♭5)

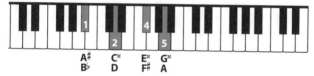

A♯   C×   E   G♯
B♭   D   F♭   A♭

B♭7(♯5)

A♯   C×   E×   G♯
B♭   D   F♯   A♭

A♯
B♭

215

Bb7(b9)

Bb7(#9)

Bb9(b5)

Bb9(#5)

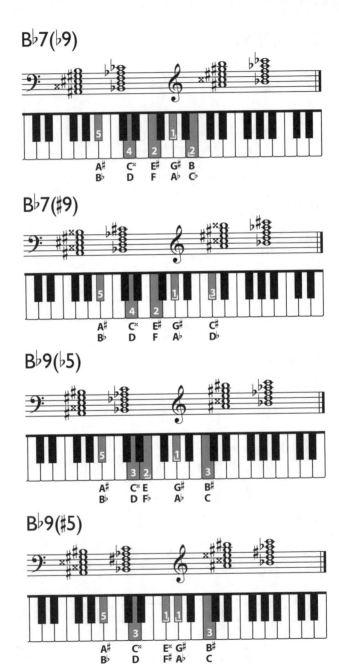

B

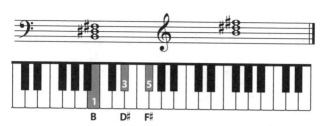

B (1ST INVERSION)

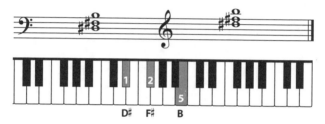

B (2ND INVERSION)

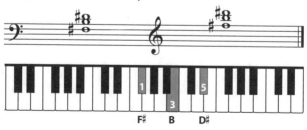

B

Bm

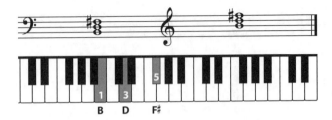

Bm (1ST INVERSION)

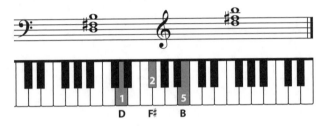

Bm (2ND INVERSION)

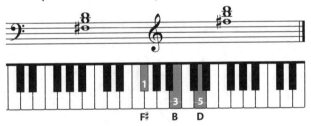

B

B°

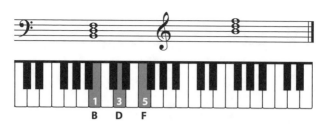

B° (1ST INVERSION)

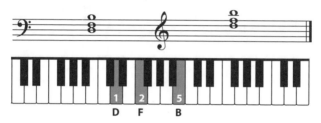

B° (2ND INVERSION)

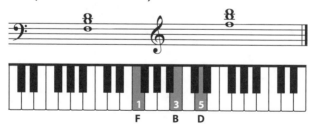

B

B+

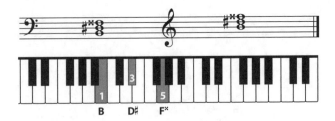

B   **D♯**   **F×**

B+ (1ST INVERSION)

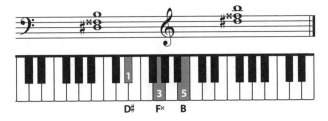

D♯   **F×**   **B**

B+ (2ND INVERSION)

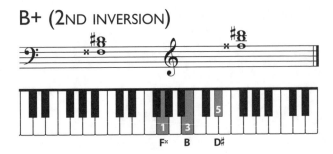

F×   **B**   **D♯**

B

Bsus2

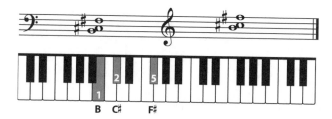

B   C#   F#

Bsus4

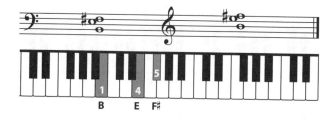

B   E   F#

B5 (POWER CHORD)

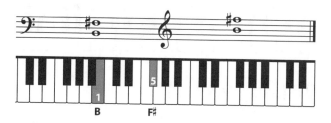

B   F#

B

B6

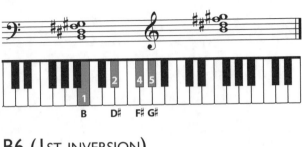

B D# F# G#

B6 (1ST INVERSION)

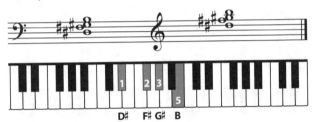

D# F# G# B

B6 (2ND INVERSION)

F# G# B D#

B6 (3RD INVERSION)

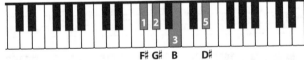

G# B D# F#

B

Bm6

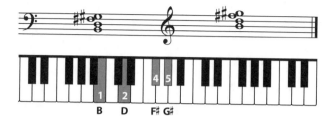

Bm6 (1ST INVERSION)

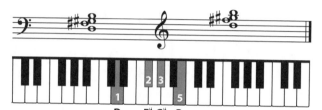

Bm6 (2ND INVERSION)

Bm6 (3RD INVERSION)

B

B7

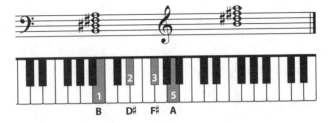

B D# F# A

B7 (1ST INVERSION)

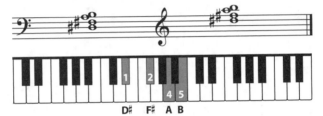

D# F# A B

B7 (2ND INVERSION)

F# A B D#

B7 (3RD INVERSION)

A B D# F#

B

Bmaj7

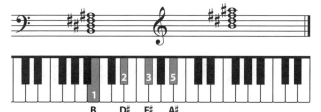

B   D#   F#   A#

Bmaj7 (1ST INVERSION)

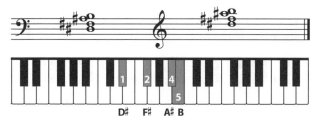

D#   F#   A# B

Bmaj7 (2ND INVERSION)

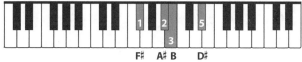

F#   A# B   D#

Bmaj7 (3RD INVERSION)

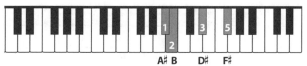

A# B   D#   F#

B

Bm7

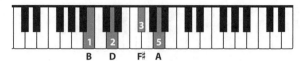

B D F♯ A

Bm7 (1ST INVERSION)

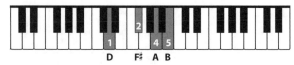

D F♯ A B

Bm7 (2ND INVERSION)

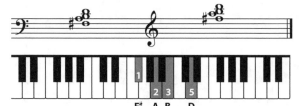

F♯ A B D

Bm7 (3RD INVERSION)

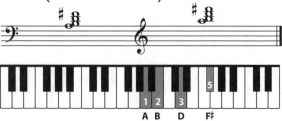

A B D F♯

B

Bm7(♭5)

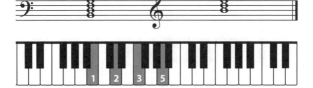

Bm7(♭5) (1ST INVERSION)

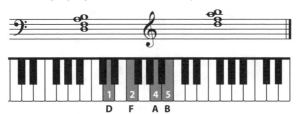

Bm7(♭5) (2ND INVERSION)

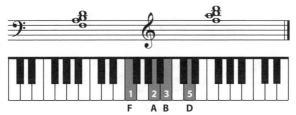

Bm7(♭5) (3RD INVERSION)

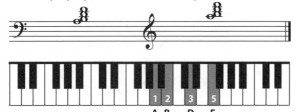

B

B°7

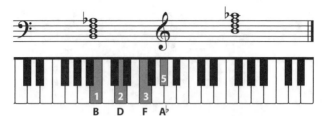

B D F A♭

B°7 (1ST INVERSION)

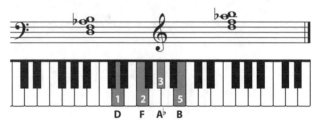

D F A♭ B

B°7 (2ND INVERSION)

F A♭ B D

B°7 (3RD INVERSION)

A♭ B D F

B

B(add9)*

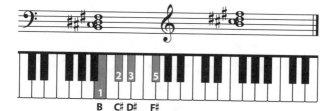

B C# D# F#

B(add9)* (1ST INVERSION)

D# F# B C#

B(add9)* (2ND INVERSION)

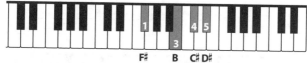

F# B C# D#

B(add9)* (3RD INVERSION)

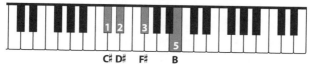

C# D# F# B

Sometimes called (add2)

B

B9

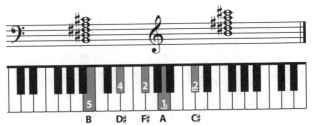

B   D#   F#   A   C#

Bmaj9

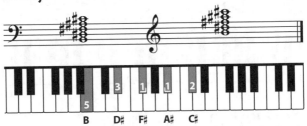

B   D#   F#   A#   C#

Bm9

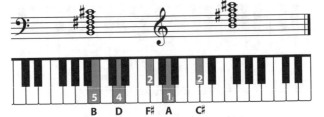

B   D   F#   A   C#